IT'S TRUE!

IT'S TRUE!

Trevor Dearing

Mohr Books

Printed by Redwood Books, Trowbridge, BA14 8RN

Published by Mohr Books
Inchmarlo Road, Banchory
Scotland AB31 4AA

First published 1996

ISBN 0 9524604 2 4

British Library Cataloguing in Publication Data.
A catalogue record for this book is available from the British Library.

Also by Trevor Dearing:

Wesleyan and Tractarian Worship (Epworth/SPCK)
Exit the Devil (Logos)
Supernatural Superpowers (Logos/Bridge USA)
Supernatural Healing Today (Logos/Bridge USA)
God and Healing of the Mind (Bridge/Valley)
A People of Power (Marshall Collins)

Also published by Mohr Books:

The Kentle-Shaddy by Eileen Mohr (novel for children aged 8-12)

A Well Brought Up Eastender by E.H. (Ernie) Relf

ACKNOWLEDGEMENTS

I could not exaggerate the thanks I owe to my darling wife, Anne, for the love, encouragement and support she has given me in the last thirty-eight years. She has been a wonderful wife and a kind and gentle mother, and also an invaluable partner in Christian ministry. I would also like to thank our four children, Rebecca, Ruth, Rachael and Philip for their love and for the enormous sacrifices they have made so that I, usually with Anne, could engage in itinerant ministry. They say that they did it for Jesus.

Then I would like to express my deep appreciation to Veronica Mansbridge for typing the manuscript - something I could not have done. I would also like to thank my editor and publisher, Eileen Mohr, for her very helpful suggestions.

I am very grateful to all our prayer partners who have held us up before the Lord, and supported us with their giving for twenty years. Then there are scores of beautiful people who have given us loving hospitality through the years of our ministry. I, with Anne, am indebted to them all. There have, too, been dozens of clergy and pastors, including bishops, who have entrusted me with ministry in their churches, fellowships and dioceses. During the years we have experienced so much trust, support and deep fellowship with so many of God's people, who have enriched our lives. Thank you to you all.

Note: The names of many people have been changed to safeguard confidentiality.

The events at St Paul's, Hainault, were first described in my book, *Exit the Devil* (1975) which has long been out of print.

CONTENTS

INTRODUCTION

"What is truth?"

This was the question that Pilate addressed to Jesus when the teacher from Galilee had been brought before him on trial for His life. It is a question which human beings have been asking from the time they first began to reason. There are, in my view, three criteria for judging whether something is or is not true.

Firstly, the statement or assertion we are asked to believe must correspond to objective reality. So, for instance, if someone came to me and said that there was an elephant in my garden, I would go to see if the statement corresponded with my senses -- could I bear witness from my own experience that this was so!

So in relation to a much more vital assertion of truth: that Jesus of Nazareth actually lived in the flesh, John wrote:

"That which was from the beginning, which we have heard, which we have seen with our eyes, which we have looked at and our hands have touched -- this we proclaim concerning the Word of life."

To the further and, humanly speaking, more unbelievable assertion that Jesus rose physically from the dead, Paul urged the importance of many witnesses to this truth:

"He appeared to Peter, and then to the Twelve. After that, he appeared to more than five hundred of the brothers at the same time, most of whom are still living, though some have fallen asleep. Then he appeared to James, then to all the apostles, and last of all he appeared to me, as to one abnormally born."

Further, when Thomas disbelieved that He had risen, Jesus said to him:

"Put your finger here; see my hands. Reach out your hand and put it into my side. Stop doubting and believe."

In fact all the main essentials of the Christian faith claim to be true because they correspond to objective, experiential facts. Can we two thousand years later believe the testimony of these first Christians as recorded in the Bible, that they had discovered objective, ultimate truth about supernatural reality? I asked myself this question from being very young: "Is Christianity true, in that there is a God, Jesus really lived, and that there is such a fact as life after death?"

A second criterion for deciding that something is true is that it coheres, fits in, with other facts that are known to be true. A simple illustration of this is that when assembling a jigsaw puzzle we know that a particular piece is right for a special place because it fits in exactly with all the other pieces that make up the complete picture. So a discerning reader of the Bible soon sees that what it proclaims as truth throughout its many pages, books and different sorts of literature is a very unified whole.

Bible teachers who have the skill of showing their listeners these many interwoven truths, linked together like a chain, build these listeners up in the belief that they are hearing ultimate truth. However, all this applies only if one believes, as fact, the first assertion of the Bible, that it was *GOD* who created heaven and earth, for the Bible nowhere actually seeks to prove the existence of God.

The third criterion of proof that something is true is, to my mind, that it *WORKS* -- it produces the results expected. This is the basis of all scientific enquiry into truth -- an experiment produces predicted results in the particular field of enquiry. Jesus, in fact, asserted that His teaching would produce results if put into practice on the conditions He imposed. His own ministry, for instance, produced results in the healing of the sick, the deliverance of captives, and transformation of lives; and He told John the Baptist's disciples that these results were evidence that He was the Messiah. Further, He predicted that these same results would occur through the ministry of His disciples:

"Anyone who has faith in me will do what I have been doing. He will do even greater things than these, because I am going to the Father."

Jesus also told parables about the Kingdom where He commended the labourers who had produced results. He further said of true believers:

"By their fruits you will know them."

In fact Jesus consistently maintained that results would always follow the proclamation of the Kingdom of God; and there has never been a time in history when mankind has looked more eagerly or more desperately for RESULTS to prove that some particular assertions are true. I realised myself, as I went into full-time Christian service, that I should see results for my ministry. Although Christianity had worked in my own life, I was aware that I was "saved" not only for my own sake, but for others too. The results I saw, the frustrations I encountered and the conclusions I have now reached are portrayed in this book.

Note: Biblical quotations are in most instances from the New International Version.

PART ONE

Seeking after truth

Chapter 1
Treasure buried in a field

They were holding me down on the kitchen table. I stopped struggling for a moment, and was suddenly filled with panic. Indescribable terror gripped me as the horrible, monstrous black thing came closer to my nose and mouth. I was eleven years old, and about to be operated on for the removal of my tonsils. As the ether was administered, I slid into merciful unconsciousness.

After the operation I was still suffering from shock, which entailed having to stay in bed for several days. Then, two weeks later, I had my first attack of groundless panic and sheer terror. These onslaughts of naked fear were to be repeated constantly in the years that followed, complicated by the onset of what is now called 'agoraphobia'. I dare not leave my parents' side even to go to school, and was terrified when left alone.

I was continually assailed by what I called a "far away feeling" when I felt to be remote from reality, and everything and everyone seemed to be a long way off. My fears switched repeatedly from the fear of death to that of going insane, or of going blind, or even of committing suicide. At night my pyjamas were often wet with perspiration as my entire body shook with terror. I constantly lapsed into periods of depression, when I felt to be in the depths of despair with a desperately heavy heart. This feeling lasted for weeks at a time. All this was extremely difficult to bear for someone not much more than a mere child.

My whole body was in sympathy with my emotions. I was very thin, pale-faced with black rings around my eyes. Diagnosed as suffering from a racing heart, I was perpetually physically ill, and as a teenager I was covered with hideous and painful spots and boils from my waist into my scalp. Even some of my hair fell out through alopecia -- all caused by the terrible stress through which I was going.

Of course, my parents sought medical help, as I did later myself, coming under psychiatric care in my teens. However, medication was unavailing at that time to help me during my repeated turbulent, sleepless nights. Mercifully I did have periods of some remission when I was able to be coaxed back to school. There I showed real intelligence and what must have been considerable ability by passing my 'School Certificate' with 'Matriculation exemption', which meant that later I could study for a London University Degree. Surprisingly perhaps, despite my frail physique and state of mind, I was very interested in sport; an interest which I have retained all my life.

It is only in retrospect that I can see that all this time, from the age of eleven, I was engaged in a spiritual pursuit for the ultimate meaning and purpose of life. I often felt that my life was only like that of an actor on a stage, playing a part, eventually to have the curtain brought down to end the charade. The kinds of questions I was asking were: "Who am I?", "Where am I going?", "Why am I here?". In my efforts to find answers I went once or twice with an old lady who lived next door to us, to St James Parish Church; but seemingly did not find what I was seeking. I asked questions about Confirmation but, at that time, the Anglican liturgical service rang no bells in my heart. Still my deepest spiritual questions were unanswered.

It was with relief that I left school at the age of sixteen. My hopes for an interesting career were somewhat dashed, however, following a medical examination. A specialist wrote to the office where I had started to work: "This young man will only be fit for light office work as long as he lives." My sickness meant in fact that I was unable to settle for long at any place of employment, even during the times when I felt somewhat better.

At the age of eighteen, like all young men at that time, I

had to have a medical examination in preparation for conscription into two years' National Service in the armed forces. This I failed conclusively, and at this time my illness became so severe that I even imagined that my parents were poisoning me, as I lapsed into a state of paranoia.

However, some of the time I managed to work, and now it was as a general clerk at the Earle's Cement Works in Hull. Here I met Ken, a young man who was a table tennis enthusiast, and I rapidly developed a keen interest in the game.

As I was rubbing the sweat off my brow with a towel, after a very energetic game, Ken said to me:

"I bet I could beat you if we played on a table in our youth club!"

"Where's that?" I enquired.

"I go to Queen's Methodist Church Youth Club in the centre of town," he replied. "Would you like to meet me there for a game? You might even get into our club team."

It was, perhaps, no coincidence that my pretty sister Audrey, who was slim and dark-haired, and fourteen months younger than myself, had also begun to go to that particular church and youth club, and that she was also inviting me to go there.

Eventually I accepted these invitations and there met the most friendly, loving and caring group of young people I had ever known. Now at just nineteen years of age, I went with them to my first ever Sunday evening service.

I sat feeling nervous and panicky in a seat near the door of the huge Central Hall, singing the hymns as well as I could, and listening to the sermon. The Reverend William D. Watts, who was preaching, eventually quoted the words of Jesus:

"Come to me, all you who are weary and burdened, and I will give you rest. Take my yoke upon you and learn from me, for I am gentle and humble in heart, and you will find rest for

your souls. For my yoke is easy and my burden is light."
These words from the New Testament seemed to enter right into
my being; into the innermost depths of my mind. They were
like rays of light piercing an inner darkness, driving away all
doubt and fear. As the preaching continued about Jesus being
the revelation of God's character I felt that the deepest questions
I had ever asked about life had been answered.

In a moment of what can only have been Divine
revelation, I knew that God existed; that He was a loving
heavenly Father; that Jesus was my Friend and Healer; that there
was hope for my healing and for my life in the future. Peace
swept over my being; a peace the like of which I had never
imagined existed. This gave way to joy, and joy gave way to
excitement. I knew that God's love was the key to unlock all
the mysteries of life and that His power was a source of healing.

On looking back I can well understand what Jesus meant
when He said that the Kingdom of Heaven was like a man
digging in a field, who unearthed a casket of incalculable
treasure. In his excitement he went away and sold all he had to
buy that field. I knew that my life could never be the same
again.

My parents, who never went to church, were the first to
witness a remarkable change in their son. I became radiantly
happy and eventually almost completely free of my mental
illness. I began to walk upright instead of with a bent back, and
cheerfully went to work. I bought a small red New Testament
from a city bookshop and avidly began to read it as I now spent
time daily in prayer.

I didn't understand who such people as the "Galatians" or
"Thessalonians" were, to whom Paul wrote, but I did find the
New Testament a book full of God's precious promises of life
and health and peace. My sleep at night was indeed peaceful, and
I also became free of physical illnesses, growing rapidly more
strong and healthy.

One morning, which I vividly remember, I was shaving in the bathroom when I heard a knock on the door. My father came in and sat on the only available seat!

"Trevor," he said, "you have found the meaning of life; you have found God. Can you help me to find Him in the same way as you have done?"

I said a simple prayer, and thus my father came to know Jesus as his Saviour and Lord; the first person in fact that I ever "led to Christ". After a while he, too, became a faithful member of Queen's Central Hall, and made rich contributions to the Men's Fellowship. My mother, too, who had had a Salvation Army upbringing, later became a member, so that we all, including my sister, became regular worshippers at the church.

Things happened quickly in my life from that time on. I began to have very strong thoughts in my mind that I ought to be a minister of the Christian Church and be a preacher, like Mr Watts, who with Deaconess Elizabeth Gillings, became my teacher in the Faith. Despite the fact that I was learning quickly about the things of God, of which I was a keen student, I at first put these thoughts out of my mind as being proud, arrogant and presumptuous.

However, one day, when I was at the youth club, Sister Elizabeth said to me:

"Trevor, have you ever thought that you ought to be a minister?"

"Yes, I have," I replied; "but isn't it silly?"

Sister Elizabeth obviously thought it far from being silly, for she became overjoyed.

"It isn't silly, Trevor!" she exclaimed. "Mr Watts and I have felt that you were called to the ministry from first knowing you. You ought to begin training at once."

So I began studying to become a Methodist Local Preacher; the first faltering steps to becoming a minister of religion. I eventually preached my first sermon to a handful of Methodist faithfuls in a small chapel, with my father in enthusiastic attendance.

It must be said, however, that my Christian faith was constantly being examined by my keen mind. The Reverend Watts and Sister Elizabeth were sincere Christians but were certainly not of what, I was later to discover, were the totally Bible-believing, fundamentalist type. Everything was rationally examined and intelligently taught in the light of modern research into truth. The Methodist Local Preachers' Course which I followed was also far from fundamentalist -- and so was I! I remember saying to Doctor Bickford, the psychiatrist who was treating me at the time:

"I don't believe in an infallible St Paul!" And I asserted, "I believe such hymns as 'I need Thee every hour' express neurosis rather than any mature expression of Christian worship."

He was very pleased to hear this, and remarked that I was grasping Christianity with reasonable thought and not from a mainly emotional need. Nevertheless, in those early two years at Queen's Hall I felt that I had discovered the truth of the ultimate meaning of human life, including my own. My future, I felt sure, was to be in the ministry of the Christian Church.

Chapter 2

"I hope they're not all like him!"

It was a year later, having passed the Local Preachers' examinations in Old Testament and New Testament studies, that I saw an advertisement in the Methodist Recorder. It read:

"Are you training for the ministry? Then why not study in the beautiful surroundings of Cliff College, in Derbyshire?"

The advertisement went on to give brief details of the course of study and particulars about where to apply for admission. I had never heard of this college, but it all sounded interesting, so I mentioned it to Sister Elizabeth and Mr Watts.

Sister Elizabeth was hesitant about my going there for some reason I did not understand, but eventually the advice came back that I should apply for entry, with Mr Watts' backing. I therefore wrote to the college applying for a place.

After a week or two the Principal, the Reverend J. Eagles, replied saying that I was accepted as a student. However, there was still one problem; I had no money, so how was I going to pay my way? When I explained my predicament to the Principal, the reply staggered me.

"Come as quickly as possible," wrote Mr Eagles. "Money isn't at all necessary to come to Cliff College."

Later I learned that the motto of the College in those days was: "Born in prayer; lives by faith."

It was in January 1954, at the age of twenty, that I travelled by bus and train and arrived at the College, which I soon discovered was not only a Bible College, but a place that trained young men to be evangelists. The Spirit at the College tended to kindle the flame of fire for God and for lost souls in the hearts of all who studied there. I had spoken enthusiastically about Jesus at the Yorkshire Electricity Board in Hull, where I had last worked; an enthusiasm that had sometimes meant misunderstanding and a mild form of persecution from some workmates. I had never before, however, heard sermons aimed at converting men, women, young people and even children, in the way I was to learn at Cliff College.

When I arrived there, I was astonished when the first young man to greet me, the College Chairman, flung his arms around me and shouted, "Hallelujah! Praise Jesus! God bless you, brother, and welcome!"

I immediately thought, "I hope they're not all like him!" I was to find, however, that he was the most moderate of the students!

Consequently I was not happy at the College, because I found my fellow students more intent on and dedicated to the Christian life and ministry than I had ever known before. All the conversation was about the things of God. Students were compelled to rise early in the morning for an hour of 'quiet time'. Spiritual songs were constantly being sung. Lectures were entirely Biblical and no one had any time for anything other than Christianity in all its length and breadth and application to spiritual life. It was like an evangelical form of monastery, even with periods of compulsory manual labour included.

Furthermore, I met 'fundamentalist' Christianity for the first time. It seemed incredible to me that these young men thought that every word of the Bible was equally true; that they believed in a personal devil; and that they thought everyone who could not remember the time at which they were so-called 'born again' was going to eternal torments in hell.

It was all too much for me at that time. I wrote to Reverend Watts:

". . . but I am unhappy here, because the students seem to me to be a lot of religious fanatics. They have gone 'over the top' as Christians and they can talk of nothing else except religion. I just can't stand it, so I have decided to leave this place and come home at the end of term."

Mr Watts replied, urging that I should try to stick it out, but I was determined that I would be returning home at the first opportunity.

The end of the term came in March, but before students were allowed home there were to be some special 'Jubilee Celebrations' at the College. As the College chapel was too small, however, these were to be held in the Calver Parish Church. I went along to the services reluctantly and unhappily.

The main visiting preacher was Reverend Maurice Barnett, a leading Methodist minister in the evangelical tradition. At the last service he announced that his theme was going to be "Full surrender" and "Entire abandonment of one's life to God."

The words he uttered pierced deep into my soul. I was challenged to the very depths about the inadequacy of my commitment to God, to His Word -- the Bible -- and in response to the love of God shown on the cross of Calvary.

"I must do something about this," I thought.

"You must do something about this," echoed Maurice Barnett.

"What can I do?" I asked in my heart.

"What can you do?" asked Reverend Barnett.

"I'll run out of the door," I replied in my mind.

"Don't run out the door," urged the preacher. "Run down here and totally abandon your life to God. Give yourself over to God as a living sacrifice. If you don't, then you will be too much in the world to enjoy God and too much in God to enjoy the world. Give yourself totally, today!"

I needed no second invitation. I didn't look around to see if anyone else was responding first to lead the way. I leapt up from my seat and literally ran down the church to the altar rail, and in the best way I knew how, I surrendered all I was and ever hoped to be, to the God who had loved, saved and healed me. Once again, as at my first experience of God's love, I was enveloped in a deep peace which felt like a cloud of glory, full of God's Presence.

This indescribable peace remained with me for weeks afterwards. Of course I wrote to Mr Watts:

"I will not be coming home after all. This place is wonderful! Praise the Lord! I've joined them in entire consecration!"

Whilst at Cliff College I went on to pass my Local Preacher examinations in theology, after which I went on a mission with the College students to the town of Pocklington in Yorkshire. Then in the summer, together with a small group of fellow students, I missioned in the North East of England.

It was whilst I was preaching at the Prudhoe Street Mission in Newcastle, on the text, "It is finished", that I first saw a man respond to my sermon. He had been living as a tramp, and he now made his way to the front of the church to give his life to the Lord. The next day I saw him washed, wearing a clean suit and going to work. It was an unforgettable thrill to be a soul winner in this way.

I came back from this mission to help other students prepare for the annual 'Derwent Convention', which was held at Cliff College every August. On these occasions people, especially young people, came in their hundreds for this week of worship, preaching and teaching. A young woman whom I saw as lovely, vivacious and pretty caught my attention. It was clear that she was deeply dedicated to the Lord, and I learned that her name was Anne, and that she came to this event every year.

On this occasion she stayed behind to help the students with their clearing up after the Convention. She, along with others, was sitting in the entrance to the Tea Hall, cleaning knives and forks when I happened to pass through. I saw her; she saw me! We immediately fell in love.

Anne and I took walks and prayed together in the following few days. She told me that she was nursing at Rampton, the top security psychiatric hospital, and she shared her Bible-believing, evangelical faith with me. We realised almost immediately that God had called us together to work for Him as husband and wife. As I look back I realise that I owe so much to my time at Cliff College; I really felt, there, that I had entered into a deeper truth which I would take with me into the future; and I had also met my future Christian wife.

Chapter 3

"I want to marry a parson"

After Anne and I met at Cliff College we began at once to share as much as possible of our spiritual life together. I, of course, told her my story and she told me hers. Because her discovery of the truth of the Christian faith was so different from mine I feel it is well worth sharing.

We were seated together at the top of Froggatt Edge, just outside the Derbyshire village of Curbar, as Anne recounted to me her early experience of God. I sat with one arm wrapped around her slim waist, looking into her large, deep brown, beautiful eyes and noticing the auburn tints in her brown hair.

"I can never remember a time when I didn't believe in God and feel Him very close to my life," she said. "Even when I was very young, and lived in Barnack, in Lincolnshire, I used to go across the road to the village church. I had to use all my strength to push the huge, heavy door open, and then I would sit in a pew, all on my own, and look up at the crucifix on the rood screen in front of me. Even though I was so young, I knew Jesus was no longer hanging on that cross. I knew He was alive, and I could know Him and talk to Him."

She went on to say that she also went regularly to Sunday School of her own volition and loved to hear the Bible's stories, especially about Jesus. Her mother and father, though not regular churchgoers, were believers, and taught her many children's hymns as she sat upon their knees.

"I remember one day when I was playing with five other little girls around the village pump. The game was about what sort of man we wanted to marry when we were grown up.

"'I want to marry a policeman!' one of them said.

"'I want to marry a doctor,' said another little girl.

13

"Then it was my turn. 'I want to marry a parson!' I said, without any hesitation. I suppose the idea developed through our local Vicar, the Reverend Nesbitt. He seemed to me to be a very kind man -- I used to wave at him through the window every morning when he was going across the road to the church. He used to visit my mother regularly, to encourage her as she struggled to bring up the family. I loved Mr Nesbitt, and his special collar meant something, I knew, something about God."

As she grew older and her family moved house from village to village, Anne would cycle several miles, often in the pitch dark of country roads, in order to sit at worship in Chapel often with just a handful of sincere village Christians.

She made friends with Methodist local preachers and their families and frequently rode side by side with the junior Minister to be at his services. She told me that she had always been a sincere and devout Christian because God's hand had been upon her from the earliest days of her life. Even in those days she saw herself as sitting in meetings in the company of hundreds of people with their arms raised, joyfully worshipping God. It was a vision that God had given her.

Anne's relationship with her Lord had, however, been brought to a point of decision for her one Sunday evening in Ketton Methodist Church, Lincolnshire. At fifteen years of age, she was listening to a young man from Exeter named Ronald Heyward. He was training to be a missionary with the Japan Evangelistic Band. That night he preached about the second coming of Jesus Christ.

"Remember the words of Jesus," he said. "One will be taken to be with Him and one will be left."

He then asked the congregation, "Where will you be on that great day? Why not make sure of your salvation and accept Jesus Christ to be your Saviour and Lord?"

He then invited those who wanted to do this to raise their

hands in response to Jesus's call. Anne knew that it was the moment for her to say 'yes' to being a disciple of Jesus for the rest of her life, and without any delay she lifted her hand as an indication of her desire. Ron Heyward truly discipled Anne, for he gave her wise counsel and advice about being a Christian and for several years wrote to her about her life with the Lord.

"I was faced with a challenge to my discipleship later on," Anne told me. "I was going out with a boyfriend who was a nice young man -- I thought he was quite attractive. But he wasn't at all interested in what I was telling him about Jesus. He didn't want to come with me to prayer meetings or other Christian meetings, even though I tried to make him understand how important Jesus was -- and is! So we parted company, but I wasn't really sorry; I couldn't compromise about my wholehearted commitment to the Lord."

I assured her that I understood how she felt, because I now had exactly the same attitude! In retrospect one can see how the foundations of Anne's future ministry were being laid, as she faced something of the demands as well as the joy of Christian service.

After a little while it had been suggested to her by adult Christian friends that she should go to Cliff College to enrich her Christian life and experience. In those days female students were not allowed, so she had applied to go on the staff there. She was overjoyed when she was accepted, and it had been the beginning of her long association with the College. Anne made many friends amongst the staff, students, and the hundreds of young people who flocked there twice a year for the preaching and teaching convention.

It was while she was at Cliff College that Anne had felt the Lord to be calling her to service in nursing, and so she had applied to Rampton Hospital, Nottinghamshire, for a training place. Thus she had begun her nursing career there at the age of eighteen. To nurse these mentally ill, deficient and in some cases criminally insane people was, to Anne, a challenge but also a joy.

She found herself to be the only 'born again' Christian on the nursing staff, but nevertheless felt emboldened to speak enthusiastically about her faith without compromise. This did not, she discovered, get in the way of real friendship with other nurses, and she was also able to teach the patients hymns and choruses, as well as talking to them about Jesus.

Anne told me how thankful she was to God that He put it into the heart of Dr Robert Porter, a senior member of the medical staff and a devout Christian, with his wife Joan, to befriend her and give her an open invitation into their home. Her Christian life had also been supported by friendships she made with mature Christians in the neighbouring town of Retford through attending Church there, as well as by her regular attendance back at the Cliff College Conventions.

It had been at one such convention that God had caused our paths to cross.* Yes, we had so much love for each other from the start, and so much now in common spiritually, that it must, we believed, all have been His perfect will.

*Note: If the reader would like to know Anne's version of these events, some recollections may be found in her book, *Privileged Gifts* (Marshall Pickering). She hopes to write a fuller memoirs with the title *Called to be a Wife*.

Chapter 4

"It's different in there!"

There were two main impediments to a natural relationship blossoming between Anne and myself after our meeting at Cliff College. The first was that the rules of the Methodist Church prohibited a man from getting married until he had undergone all his training and had been ordained. In my case this meant a wait of almost seven years. The prospect looked bleak: it promised to be an extremely difficult period for two people in their early twenties who had fallen head over heels in love, and who felt called to serve the Lord together. Secondly I had to go and minister for one year as a "lay student-pastor" in a rural Methodist circuit of churches in Norfolk, whilst Anne was training to be a nurse at Rampton Hospital in Retford.

It was thus with heavy hearts that we bade farewell to each other, as Anne boarded a train at Sheffield station on her way back to continue her work and studies.

I arrived at Melton Constable in Norfolk to begin my work there, in charge of ten small village churches, in September 1954, just before my twenty-first birthday. Lodgings had been found for me with two elderly but deeply Christian spinsters; and so my first task as a pastor in the Aylsham, Briston, Reepham Circuit began.

In order to pass my examinations for entry into a Methodist Theological College I would have to do a great deal of studying, and yet I had considerable responsibility, for a young man of my age, in ministering to the godly Methodist people who in small numbers attended those scattered churches. I went to serve these people with all the Bible-believing, evangelistic enthusiasm I had entered into at Cliff. I would, I thought, minister all the truth I had recently learned. A test of

17

its veracity would surely be: would it bear fruit in a rural Methodist circuit?

I did, however, have an extremely pleasant surprise on my arrival in Norfolk, which proved to be an incalculable help for me in what otherwise would have been a very lonely situation. I had no sooner arrived there when Anne wrote to me with the news that she was leaving Rampton Hospital to nurse in Norfolk, eventually to work at Kelling Sanatorium, near Holt -- only five miles from Melton Constable! My heart leapt with elation as I read these words.

So the relationship between us was able to grow and develop, after all. It was still not always easy for us to meet with one another owing to our lack of transportation and our respective duties, but it was certainly better than either of us had once expected, and we were able sometimes to serve the Lord together in those rural churches, as we met with the Lord's people.

Often I had to cycle twenty miles on totally dark roads to minister in those churches, but nothing could dampen my evangelistic enthusiasm. I even invited two Cliff College evangelists to conduct a ten-day mission in my two churches at Briston, and was delighted with the result: three people gave their hearts to the Lord. I started a "Christian Endeavour" group and encouraged Bible study and prayer meetings, which were attended by at least a few of the believers.

Our time in Norfolk was memorable in many ways, but especially for the conversion of a young married woman called Rosemary. It was remarkable from several points of view. I first met Rosemary in very unusual circumstances.

One Sunday morning I was preaching at Hall Street Methodist Church in Briston. My subject was the call and conversion of Peter the fisherman (Matthew 4: 18-22). I had finished the service, and when I walked out of the church into the porch, I was startled to find a woman there who was sobbing almost uncontrollably.

"What's the matter?" I asked in concern.

"I'm too unclean to come into Church," replied Rosemary, trying to suppress her sobs. "I've had an illegitimate child by a man other than my husband, and the Vicar says I and my child are spiritually dirty, and he won't baptise my baby. But I've been listening to your sermon through the cracks in the door. I heard every word you said, and I wish I could know Jesus as my Saviour and Lord."

"You can know Him *now*," I urged. "If only you ask Him into your heart and life by saying a simple prayer."

I then led Rosemary in the "Sinner's Prayer", acknowledging sin, repenting of it and asking Jesus to be her Saviour.

As I was reflecting that we are all dirty in the eyes of our holy God unless we have been cleansed through faith in what He did for us on Calvary, Rosemary said:

"I feel a deep peace filling my whole being. I feel I really do know Jesus now, in a personal way -- it's wonderful! I believe He has taken away all my sins; I've got real peace with God, now."

"Yes, Jesus *is* wonderful!" I agreed.

"Would you be kind enough to come and pay us a visit, please?" she asked. "My husband's an alcoholic -- he gets into terrible tempers when he's been drinking; it's awful -- he shouts and raves at me and the children, and knocks me about if I don't keep out of his way. He scares us to death when he's like that.

"If only he could come to know the Lord, as I've done. What a difference it could make to us all!"

I made one or two tactful enquiries about the family from Christians in the neighbourhood and learned that the rows and arguments, screams and shouting which came through the doors and windows were indeed well known in the area.

When I later visited the home, as I had promised, I found

a most remarkable willingness on the part of the husband, Bob, to listen to the Gospel.

"I've seen such a change in my wife," he explained, "there must be something in it. She's suffered terribly with her nerves in the past, and now she seems so peaceful and well; please explain what has happened to her."

He accepted Jesus as his Lord and Saviour at that first visit, and soon began to testify to his workmates about what Jesus had done for him, especially the fact that he had been completely delivered from alcoholism.

Weeks later, when I was paying yet another visit to the home, I was met at the front gate by one of Rosemary and Bob's children, a boy who was about five years of age.

"Hello Pastor Dearing," was his greeting. Then, pointing towards the front door, he said, "It's different in there! It's different in there! You see, we're very happy now. Jesus has come to live in our house and it's different in there."

People in the neighbourhood also expressed their surprise at the wonderful change that had taken place in that home, which was now a home of peace and love. It was the first instance we had witnessed of the way in which Jesus can transform marriages and homes, in fact the whole domestic scene, when He is invited into the situation.

Our work in Norfolk, for all its difficulties, was obviously not without fruit for the Lord. I certainly had not been used by God to bring Christian revival in these churches, and the church membership had not increased, but I had seen the power of the Gospel at work in at least two lives, and this seemed to me to be proving its truth.

Anne and I both left Norfolk in the late July of 1955, and our first meeting point was back again at the Cliff College 'Derwent Convention'. But now there were young people from the Queen's Hall in Hull, who had come for the first time due to my insistence. They now found and acquired that particular evangelical fervour which emanated from the Spirit's presence in that holy place.

I had, by now, been accepted for training as a Methodist minister, and had elected to study at Wesley Theological College, Headingley, Leeds. It was September 1955 when I arrived there and Anne, in order that we might be together, again moved hospitals, this time to nurse at St George's, Rothwell.

Her dedicated Christian nursing was rewarded by her winning Matron's Prize for Nursing Ethics and Sister Tutor's prize for First Aid and Hygiene. Anne also found the Matron of the hospital to be a very sincere, evangelical Christian, and she it was who introduced Anne to the Inter Hospital Nurses' Christian Fellowship which, together with Church in Leeds, was further to nurture her Christian life.

Chapter 5

"So much the worse for the Bible!"

My chosen theological college at Headingley soon proved to be very different from Cliff College; as different, in fact, as could be imagined. Here at Wesley College the emphasis was almost entirely on academics, and I was immediately entered for a London University External Degree in Divinity.

The lectures were varied and were based on human reasoning about every conceivable subject related to Christianity. The lecturers approached all their teaching from this point of view, although it was evident that they were all sincere Christians -- albeit of a very different variety from that found at 'Cliff'. There were lectures on 'Pastoral Theology' which were aimed at teaching the practicalities of being a Methodist minister, and there were daily prayers and weekly services in the College Chapel, but they were not where the weight of the curriculum was placed.

The emphases in Biblical Studies were first of all on the learning of Hebrew and New Testament Greek, which gave deep insight into the meaning of the original text, and would later help in expounding the Scriptures. Apart from this we were initiated into what is called Lower and Higher Criticism of the books of the Bible.

Lower Criticism was straightforward. It was based on the fact that, for instance, there are no actual fully complete gospels as they were originally written, but that our present gospels are the expert putting together of varieties of writings in ancient manuscripts; so the renderings can vary. For this reason, we were told, the ending of Mark's Gospel, from Chapter 16 verses 9-20, must be regarded as a later addition to the original, as they do not appear in the oldest manuscripts.

Higher Criticism was much more radical. We were led to examine the Pentateuch -- the first five books of the Old Testament -- traditionally ascribed to Moses. From archaeological evidence it seems that there were centuries of the early stories of Genesis being passed on orally from generation to generation before they were actually written down by scribes. Then, we were taught, there were at least four different authors; one who used 'Jehovah' as the name of God; one who used the name 'Elohim'; a Law School which wrote Deuteronomy and applied a principle of reward and punishment even to the Israelite kings; and finally a priestly code which appeared in Leviticus and Chronicles.

We were shown that there were two creation stories in Genesis and two different accounts of the Hebrew conquest of Canaan; a slow conquest in Judges and a rapid one in Joshua. The prophetic writings were proved to be of genuine authorship except for Isaiah, to which, we were taught, had been added utterances by two later prophets beginning at Chapter 40. The book of Job was described as a long poem on the meaning of suffering.

The New Testament had fared little better at the hands of the 'Higher Critics'. Mark was seen to be the first gospel to be written. This young man was in fact a disciple of Peter. Matthew and Luke were seen to have incorporated much of Mark's gospel into their writings and also to have used another common source which experts called 'document Q'. Then they had their own particular material.

We were told that Matthew, who was not the disciple, had added his material especially to convince Jews that Jesus fulfilled ancient prophecy and was their Messiah; whilst Luke, the friend of Paul, had written for Gentiles. John's Gospel, we were told, was also not written by the disciple, but was a later work, not emphasising historical fact but the theological meaning of Jesus

Christ's life.

The Letters ('Epistles') were taught as being of genuine authorship but style and theological teaching were said to show that the so-called Second Letter of Peter was not by the apostle; nor were the Letters to the Ephesians, Colossians, Hebrews, 1 and 2 Timothy and Titus considered to be written by Paul. All this and the differences in detail of the accounts in the gospels, overthrew, we were told, all belief that the New Testament was dictated, as it were, to the authors by God and that every word was infallible. There was no place for fundamentalism at Wesley College.

The lecturer in Theology, the Reverend Raymond George, was a man who soon won my admiration and affection. Although he, I am sure, accepted the insights of Higher and Lower Criticism, he was essentially Biblical in his teaching. He was, in fact, a Biblical theologian who regarded the Bible as the basis of Christian truth. We were taught, we debated, and some students even argued about the fundamental doctrine of the Christian faith.

I was thrilled, as part of my degree course, to be studying the Biblical, historical and contemporary teaching about what Jesus actually accomplished by His death on the cross. Basically this fell into four categories of thought. There was first the concept that Jesus was a *substitute* provided by the Father to prevent His wrath against sin falling on us. Then there was the *representative* concept: that Jesus was the perfect representative and the perfect mediator between sinful mankind and a holy God. We also studied the *victory* concept: that Jesus fought and won a battle between sin, the law and the Devil on the one hand and sinful mankind on the other. The *ransom* concept portrayed Jesus as giving Himself as a ransom to the Devil in order to pay the price of man's release from his clutches. All these thoughts were enveloped in the truth that God showed His infinite love for lost mankind by giving His Son to die on Calvary. I, personally, accepted all Raymond George's basic teaching as true except for the idea that Jesus actually stood between the wrath of God falling upon man, pleading to the Father not to let His vengeance fall upon us.

"This can't be true!" I called out in class.

"It's in the Bible!" replied Mr George.

"Then," I impulsively retorted, "it's so much the worse for the Bible!"

I was now using my reason to analyse theology in my search for truth, not just slavishly accepting everything as truth because of one aspect of teaching; this time as it appeared in the Letter to the Hebrews. I was becoming what is known as a 'Liberal' theologian. I had moved away from the Fundamentalism of Cliff College. To me God was pure Love; a father, not a medieval despot; and this, I believed, was summed up in Paul's words: "God was in Christ, reconciling the world to himself" (2 Cor. 5 v 19).

In our three years of being lectured in theology we did not, however, touch at all on topics such as 'The Signs of Christ's Coming'. 'The Nature of the Antichrist' or 'The Place of Israel in the Plan of God'. All these subjects were regarded by Reverend George, if I understood him right, as the interests of the 'Protestant Underworld'.

Church History was also a most illuminating part of the course which we studied at Wesley College. It was, for instance, very challenging to learn of all that the early Christians withstood in the various forms of persecution and cruel death rather than deny the Lordship of Jesus. We saw how the liturgy developed; how the time and manner of baptism changed with the passing of decades; how the ministry became that of bishops, priests and deacons; how the Canon of Scripture was put together by Church Councils amidst the many competing books claiming to be written by the Apostles.

We traced the development of doctrine about the manhood

and divinity of Christ, culminating in the formulation of the doctrine of the Trinity. We watched the gradual ascendancy of the Church at Rome, the division of the Church into East and West, and were dismayed at the loss of ancient Christian cities and countries to Islam.

As a further part of my degree course I studied also the main principles of the other major world religions. Whilst seeing some truth in them, I became ever more thankful that I was a Christian! I also studied Philosophy, learning of the thought of great non-Christian, mainly atheistic teachers down the centuries. 'Psychology' and 'Psychology of Religion' let us into the work of such people as Freud and Jung; the development of religious consciousness; and an analysis of the mental process of conversion.

Thus our education was deep and wide as we were prepared to go out into the world as knowledgeable men, ready to meet the questions of learned and unlearned alike. My own grasp of the truth as thinkers have seen it to be had become remarkably informed, and I had been encouraged to think out my faith and put it on firm foundations with my God-given mind.

At Wesley College I earned in the end also my Bachelor of Divinity Degree from London University. I had been very happy in my relationship with other students and engaged them in lively theological debate. Throughout the period at Wesley College I was also able to maintain my prayer life and deep commitment to the Lord. In vacations I had to work -- as a postman, nursing auxiliary and even an engineer's labourer -- as I received no grant from the Local Education Authorities for my training, and I had to add this secular work to my studies in order to manage financially. Nevertheless, Anne and I saw quite a lot of each other, and, if it were possible, fell even more deeply in love and even more convinced that we were called to serve the Lord together.

Our relationship was strained at times, however, and we felt that we couldn't always handle it, because our love for each other was so strong; and yet we were determined to maintain our purity and all the Christian standards of morality. Fulfilment and relief eventually came in what was a most unexpected turn of events. The Methodist Conference completely overturned their 'marriage' rule at one stroke. It was announced that men offering for the Ministry could be married at any time!

With the potential support of my father, therefore, we were married almost immediately at Barn Hill Methodist Church in Anne's home town of Stamford, and took up our abode in a bed-sitter in Leeds about two miles from Wesley College. I, however, still had to live in the College during term time. . . I must admit, though, that I did rather flout the rules. I came home out of the College every night to sleep at the bed-sit, and early every morning walked bravely back past the Principal's house. He must have seen me, but turned a blind eye to what I was doing. He proved to be human! However, at the last College meeting of the year he did say to the students, with a smile:

"I have never been one to believe much in miracles, but there has been one this year. Trevor Dearing has slept in his bed for three terms without ever disturbing the sheets!"

It was a happy note on which to leave Leeds and journey to my first appointment as a 'Probationary Minister' at Brighouse in West Yorkshire. We took up residence in the furnished manse and Anne was already eight months pregnant -- "great with child," we joked, in the quaint words of the King James version.

Chapter 6

This is my body . . . This is my blood. . .

As I look back I can see that by this time in my spiritual pilgrimage I had had an experience of God at the age of nineteen which had brought me a great deal of wholeness in spirit, mind and body. I had also been exposed at Cliff College to an evangelical and fundamentalist interpretation of the faith and I had seen the power of the Gospel message to work a revolution in human life; I had seen the value of emphasising a specific commitment to the person of Jesus Christ as Lord. I had also encountered at Wesley College a more liberal, but nevertheless, Biblical approach and knew the value of exercising one's intellect in understanding Christianity. Now I was to encounter the 'Catholic' faith and embrace a great deal of that particular view of the truth. I believe that in all this, the Spirit of God was guiding me into truth. This particular encounter was to take place in the small West Yorkshire town of Brighouse.

It was in fact only two weeks after our arrival at Brighouse that Anne began to experience pains in her back. Although she had still a month to go before our baby was due we felt it wise to call the doctor. He decided to admit her into hospital for observation. The next morning I phoned the ward:

"How is my wife, Mrs Dearing?" I asked.

"We have a surprise for you," answered the Ward Sister.

"Oh, has our baby been born early?" I enquired.

"No!" was the startling reply. "You are the father of twins!"

Anne herself had not known that there were two babies until the first one had been delivered. What a surprise; twin girls! Now we faced a problem, for the pram we had bought and all our preparations had been for one child! What hard work these delightful baby girls proved to be, especially as they wouldn't feed properly and they also were waking each other up continually during the night! Somehow we coped, though we were now far from the help of relatives who all lived many miles away.

I had charge of three churches at this stage and the people were helpful. They arranged an American style 'Baby Shower' which brought in dozens of gifts. Also one day, Sarah, an unmarried lady from Clifton Methodist Church, came to offer regular weekly help in the home. Anne was determined to be a good Minister's wife and, as we had no car, she pushed the new heavily built twin pram up hill and down dale in order to cover the three mile walk to church.

I still had a great deal of studying to do as part of my training for the ministry. I was in my study all morning and out on my bicycle every afternoon visiting or taking meetings, so they were busy days.

I still maintained my evangelistic enthusiasm from Cliff College, although I was now much more academic. My enthusiasm came across in my sermons and in my suggestions for Circuit missions. This emphasis, however, was not well received by the Methodist officials. The Stewards -- the senior laymen who had invited us to the Circuit -- soon began to object.

"We believe in evangelism by teaching," they told me, and after a while they began to criticise me by saying, "We want a social Gospel, none of this Cliff College evangelism for us. We don't want that sort of approach in our churches."

Things were beginning to prove difficult for us in our work and witness, as not only officials, but many of the "respectable" Methodists in the nine churches in which I had to preach were also reacting adversely to the challenge.

Added to this I found the Methodist Circuit system of three ministers preaching around nine churches on Sundays very frustrating. Ministerial appointments were allocated according to

how much money each church put into the circuit kitty, and as
I had pastoral charge of three of the smallest churches, I didn't
often preach in any of them. This meant that I didn't have a
regular preaching appointment in one church, through which I
could follow up my new pastoral contacts by inviting people to
hear me preach at my own church. I was finding the Methodist
circuit system very hard to handle from an evangelistic point of
view, especially as the Methodism I had known at Queen's Hall
in Hull was under the jurisdiction of the Methodist Home
Missions Department. It was known as 'Mission Methodism'
and operated under a different system from 'Circuit Methodism'
in that the minister had only one church, which was a base for
evangelistic activity. I became more and more frustrated, and I
also became utterly exhausted with trying to exercise an evangelistic ministry in a 'Circuit' situation; so that eventually I came
near to breakdown. I shared my problems with the senior
minister of West Yorkshire, the Reverend Harold Keys, Chairman of the District.

"Your place is in Mission Methodism," declared Harold
Keys, very firmly. "That is where you ought to go when your
training is complete and you are ordained in a year's time. I'll
see what I can do to help you."

After a few weeks, however, he came back to me explaining that he had been unsuccessful in finding me a place in
Mission Methodism and he urged me to try to help myself by
contacting senior 'Mission' ministers. I did this, only to be told
that I stood no chance of obtaining a place in Mission Methodism, because I "didn't know the right people".

I was dumbfounded. Was this the way the officials of the
Methodist Church sought God's will and purpose for one of
their ministers? I was further upset when my own Circuit
Superintendent Minister was virtually sacked from his post by
the Circuit Quarterly Meeting and had to leave one year before
he was due to retire. It was all so unedifying.

Another development had been taking place in our lives, parallel to all these disappointments. I had been in a lot of contact with the Reverend John Lister, the Vicar of Brighouse, and his three curates, whose deep spirituality I much admired. They certainly were sincere Christians, who had only one parish church as a centre of their work, devotion and mission. This, I saw, was the basis of the Anglican system. Also, through their witness, I was coming much more to appreciate the meaning and significance of the Sacrament of Holy Communion as the main act of worship for believing Christians. I spent a great deal of time with John Lister discussing what Jesus meant when He had said, "This is my body and this is my blood, do this in remembrance of me." I saw that this was a material and tangible means by which we came to Jesus and through which He came to us.

I felt discontented with the way in which this supreme act of Christian devotion was occasionally tacked on to the end of a Methodist preaching service. I was also much impressed by the richness of Anglican liturgical services as I joined with the clergy at their early morning devotions. Then through my meeting with other deeply spiritual Anglicans at Clergy and Ministers' fraternals, I began to realise that in ecumenical debates I was more on the side of the Anglicans than I was the Methodists!

I had not yet been ordained as a Methodist minister and I began to doubt that I ever should be, because I had begun to question the validity of Methodist Orders in the Church Catholic. I was sure that we couldn't just start churches as the Methodists had done after the death of John Wesley. My studies of John Wesley himself had shown him to be a man of deep sacramental persuasion, a life-long Anglican.

Anne and I prayed about this and discussed it seemingly endlessly. Although Anne had been converted in a Methodist church, she had actually been confirmed in the Church of England as a young girl, and she had been much attracted to the

Church when a child at Barnack. She only wanted the best for me, although she was very much still of evangelical persuasion. She eventually said that she was willing to go into the Church of England ministry with me if I felt I would be happier there.

Through the good offices of the Vicar, John Lister, I had more than one interview with the Bishop of Wakefield, who without any hesitation said that he would accept me as an Anglican clergyman if I would go to a Church of England Training College for one year. We realised that we faced real hardship to do this as a family, but we decided that it was right for us to make the transition.

I was confirmed in Brighouse and announced my resignation from the Methodist Ministry in July 1960. We got ready to go to Birmingham where I had been granted a place at Queen's Anglican Theological College. In our two years at Brighouse we had not seen one person converted to Christ.

We faced many practical and financial difficulties as well as emotional ones as we arrived at an empty curate's house in Stockland Green, Birmingham in the July of that year. We had lived at Brighouse in a furnished manse and so we were without even a table to eat off or a bed to sleep in. We were a family of five as, at this time, we were also looking after Anne's aged father. John Lister had tried to come to our help. He had given us the bird table which had been in his garden to use for dining. Anne scrubbed it clean and put a cloth on it, and this, together with four wooden chairs from the Parish Hall, made up the dining suite. A Vicar at Clifton had given us an old lounge suite, and we had disused hospital beds on which to sleep. Our dressing table consisted of three suitcases placed on top of each other and covered with a cloth. So, one way or another we improvised with furnishings.

On her way to the house, travelling through Birmingham by bus, whilst I went in the small removal van containing a few possessions, Anne had seen a piece of linoleum being sold off cheap. She thought, "That looks a nice piece of lino. I must have a closer look."

So she dismounted from the bus with the two-year-old twins to check it out. Yes, it was a real bargain, so she spent the last of her savings on it.

It was heavier than she had anticipated, but she struggled with it to the bus stop, encouraging the twins to toddle along at her side.

As she was about to board the bus with her new acquisition plus the little twins, she was dismayed to hear the conductor shout:

"Sorry lady -- you can't bring that on this bus -- it's too big!" Whereupon he signalled a double ring on the bell, and the bus pulled away!

The same thing happened with the next bus; and the next . . . But eventually, just as Anne was beginning to give up hope of ever covering a floor with her bargain, in her next attempt to struggle onto a bus, she found herself being helped with the lino and the twins, instead of being rebuffed.

"I'm not really s'posed to let anybody on the bus with anything as big as that," commented this warm-hearted conductor, "but there's plenty o' room at the moment, so it's not doin' any 'arm 'ere. I'll keep an eye on it for you."

Thus she staggered to the house carrying our first floor covering. It was becoming the first home we had to call our own. We were being financed by a grant from the Church Commissioners, by another from the Church Times 'Train-a-Priest' fund, and by the Bishop of Wakefield's Discretionary Account, but it wasn't enough even for basic requirements. So Anne went off to nurse three nights a week. She had to leave the children in the care of her father during the times I was at College because at that time no married students were allowed to sleep at home. I also worked as an assistant nurse at a psychiatric hospital during vacations. One way or another we got through.

Whilst at the Anglican College I studied for a Master of
Arts Degree at Birmingham University, writing a thesis on
'Wesleyan and Tractarian Worship' which was later published --
my first book. At Queen's College I learned much about the
nature of the Sacraments, about the value of periods of quiet
retreat in the Christian life, about the use of Daily Offices as a
basis for devotion, and the place of meditation in the life of
prayer. I even began to make my Confession in the presence of
a priest, as I saw this to be entirely Scriptural and a means of
great release for a Christian (James 5 v 6; John 20 v 23). Queen's
Theological College had a strong devotional emphasis for those
who were training there. It was, however, a hard and difficult
year, when we drew closer to the Lord and to each other in our
determination to win through. It was with relief at Easter 1961
that we learned that the Bishop of Wakefield had appointed me
to be a Curate in the parish of Todmorden on the borders of
Yorkshire and Lancashire, and that Anne could move into the
empty Curate's house with her father and the children. We were
grateful in the move for the help of the 'Poor Clergy Relief
Fund' who sent us money and clothes. We also now began to
have a reasonable salary at last.

Before we left Birmingham, however, we had a real test of
our calling to the ministry of the Church presented to us.
During the Easter vacation I had gone to work in the office of
a firm of jewellery case makers in order to earn some more
money. The accountant of this particular firm had run off with
some money and left the books in a particularly bad state. I,
who had gained knowledge of accountancy when in Hull, was
able to straighten everything out, much to the delight of the
Managing Director who owned the company.

"Are you really serious about going into the ministry of
the Church?" he asked me.

"Yes, I am," I replied. "Why do you ask?"

"Because, if you would stay on here I would make you a Director on a high salary, and one day I would pass the whole Company over to you, as I have no children," he explained.

He went on to say that he would give me until 6.00 pm on the following Sunday to make up my mind about whether to accept the offer. He would telephone our home to find out the answer to his proposition.

I arrived home excitedly to tell Anne the news.

"Whatever shall we do?" I exclaimed. "It would be a change from our very poor financial situation and guarantee our future."

I named the starting salary which was, to us, a small fortune. Anne, however, was immediately adamant.

"You are called, Trevor, to the ministry of the Church," she affirmed. "You are as surely called by God as anyone ever has been. No! We will win through this difficult period and although we may be always financially poorer we shall be spiritually richer. 'What shall it profit a man if he gain the whole world and lose his own soul?'"

Of course I was in agreement, and once again thankful for such a wonderful wife. We had put our hand to the plough and there was no looking back. We had decided long before the Managing Director called -- it was to be on and on in the full-time service of the Lord. The temptation to leave had been faced and overcome. It was thus with strengthened resolve that we arrived to begin our work with myself as a Curate in the parish of Todmorden. I was made a Deacon by the Bishop of Wakefield at Michaelmas 1961 and ordained Priest in Wakefield Cathedral on Trinity Sunday 1962. We were now in the Anglican ministry!

Chapter 7

"Anglicans we are and Anglicans we remain!"

Todmorden is a small town on the borders of Yorkshire and Lancashire, on the very edge of the diocese of Wakefield, where I was ordained. It is set deep in a valley, with hills rising on every side. The surrounding landscape is very barren, with a peculiar kind of ruggedness and beauty all its own. However, it proved to be a very damp and cold place in which to live.

The Vicar, Reverend Harry Hodgson, his wife and family, together with all the parishioners, gave us a very warm welcome, and we were pleased to discover that the parish had completely refurbished and redecorated the Curate's house where we were to live. It was a terraced house with no garden, and two of the five bedrooms were in the attic. Anne set about making it really homely and we settled happily in the house as a family of five. I was able to use one of the attic rooms as a study, where I finished off my Master's Degree for Birmingham University. This, my examination of Wesleyan and Tractarian worship, was intended to show how an evangelical emphasis and a catholic view of the Sacraments could be closely inter-related.

There were two congregations in the parish, which were not exactly opposed to one another but rarely met together. The situation had arisen because there were two church buildings: the large parish church which was of Victorian style, and the older St Mary's Church which was in the town centre. Apparently it had been hoped to close St. Mary's when the parish church was built, but a section of the people refused to move, and carried on as a worshipping congregation.

I was not given charge of St. Mary's Church as I had hoped, but was under the jurisdiction of the Vicar in all things and had to assist him at both churches. I found, however, that my Biblical and evangelical emphasis in preaching was particularly well accepted at St Mary's. We formed several friendships in the town, including a good relationship with the local Police Inspector and his wife.

I felt strongly called to try to win the young people of the parish for Christ and so began a Youth Club in order to get alongside them. I soon found, however, that the young people from the local Grammar School, who were the first members of the Club, and the young people of the Secondary Modern School, just would not mix together. I made an observation to this effect in the presence of a young local newspaper reporter, who then wrote an article about the division in the weekly paper. It was a time when there was much discussion going on nationally about the desirability of Comprehensive education, and soon the national press began to highlight the situation at Todmorden as an example of the bad effect of separating young people into two different schools and forms of education.

It was not long before television crews were out on the streets of Todmorden questioning local residents about what had become a national talking point. It was my first taste of media publicity, and I didn't like it! The Vicar said that it had done the parish "no good"! Certainly it did not result in the conversion of any of the young people!

I was also given the opportunity to minister amongst children, especially as the local Primary and Infants School was of Church of England foundation, and I went in to teach the catechism and take assemblies. I also taught English and General Studies at the local College of Further Education, the income from which helped along the family budget. Anne was, of course, very occupied in the home as wife and mother, but did not miss out at all on attendance with the family at Church.

I was regarded as being in a learning position, and it was the Vicar's task to help me further to make the transition from being a Methodist to being an Anglican clergyman. When the

Vicar and I prayed together, therefore, it was a straightforward matter of going through the Prayer Book Office of Mattins and Evensong which I found most edifying. There was, however, no prayer for the salvation of souls or the building up of the Kingdom of God in the town. Reverend Harry Hodgson was a member of the local Rotary Luncheon Club and also a Freemason. He seemed to have no interest in evangelism. One day I tentatively broached the subject of having a Church Army Mission to the parish.

"Trevor!" exclaimed the Vicar. "The times of the services are on the notice board, the church doors are open, and I am here in my stall to take the Service. Those who want to come can do so, and those who don't can stay away."

We had hardly been in Todmorden for more than a year, however, when the twins became sick. They developed chronic and acute asthma and the doctor frequently had to be sent for to come and help them to breathe. I too developed the same complaint and was referred to a specialist.

"It's this cold, damp valley," explained a caring Mrs Doris Hodgson. "It's renowned for chest complaints. You'll suffer as long as you stay here."

We, as parents, were certainly not going to tolerate this sickness, especially in our children, for an indefinite period; and so I explained to the Bishop that the valley was seriously affecting our health. I even applied for a position as a Curate at Chandler's Ford in the south of England. The Bishop, however, was not wanting to lose me from the Diocese.

"You are now already well equipped to be a Vicar," he told me. "I will find you a parish as soon as possible."

He was true to his word and I was inducted as Vicar of the villages of Silkstone and Silkstone Common, near Barnsley, in January 1963, only seven months after having been ordained a priest.

We set up home in the small, modern vicarage which had

been built apparently in the grounds of a huge old one that had been demolished a few years before we arrived. The church itself was a beautiful, indeed magnificent building, dating back to the thirteenth century, its main feature being a splendid tower which housed a lovely peal of bells. It was situated at one end of the village of Silkstone and about three miles from the other village of Silkstone Common.

Silkstone itself had been a Yorkshire coal mining village and its old, small houses bore witness to the hard days of the industrial revolution. There is even a memorial in the churchyard which commemorates a mining tragedy, when a flood killed all the workers who were below ground. It is chilling to see that the ages of the miners ranged from six to twelve years.

Another monument bore an amusing inscription: "Relations and friends as you pass by -- as you are now so once was I. As I am now so you must be. Prepare for death and follow me!"

In more recent times two housing estates had been built which were quite attractively landscaped. The village of Silkstone Common, which was reached from the church by travelling through Silkstone and then up a steep hill, bore no marks of the period of coal mining and was much more residential in character. The parish had a small mission hut of prefabricated structure in this village, but it was rarely used.

Rebecca and Ruth, our twins, were now reaching school age and began their primary education; first at the Church of England School at Silkstone and then, when it closed, they were transferred to the Council's Infants' School at Silkstone Common. We were a very happy family and it was whilst we were at Silkstone that Anne gave birth to Rachael, our third daughter.

The church life was beset with problems right from the start; a battle raged around the truth of the alleged misbehaviour

of our predecessor. He had introduced very high church
spirituality and rituals, to this previously 'middle of the road'
village church which some of the worshippers liked and the
others abhorred.

The main morning service had become the Eucharist, when
some wanted Mattins. He had brought in such symbols of
'catholic' worship as a cope and a sanctus bell, and I was told
that incense had sometimes been used. A time for hearing
'Confession' was announced on the church notice board, but in
the three years we were there only one person asked on one
occasion for his confession to be heard.

The sacrament was reserved in a Tabernacle -- after the
Roman Catholic fashion -- in a new chapel, and worshippers had
been taught to genuflect to the Presence of the Lord in
sacrament on their way into and out of church. Some did this,
whilst others literally fell over their legs! I loved the 'Catholic'
emphasis but found all this hard to get used to, as I had never,
as a priest, been trained even as how to wear vestments.
Nevertheless, we were there by the Bishop's directive and we
endeavoured to do our best.

We were at first frequently invited out to dinner In
people's homes. However, we discovered that there was an
ulterior motive in this, as both sides in the parish divide wanted
to put their case to us about how bad, or conversely, how good,
the previous vicar had been. The situation was not helped by
the fact that some church leaders alleged that our predecessor had
been guilty of the misappropriation of money and not paying
debts. Once a debt collector did call at the vicarage door seeking
the priest who had now gone away!

At Church Council meetings the 'fors' and 'againsts' sat on
different sides of the room and it was not long before battle was
joined.

I discovered that the Churchwardens, the Church Secretary
and the Treasurer had all been called to see the Bishop before I

had been appointed to the parish, in an endeavour to bring peace, but it had been of no avail. At my induction as Vicar, when the Bishop had said that he knew what had been going on in the parish, no one was in the dark except myself, the innocent new incumbent. We realised later that our main task here was to bring peace to this troubled church.

By the end of the first of our three years there, much of my previous evangelistic zeal had been drained away. It would have been wonderful had the 'Catholic' spirituality of the parish genuinely been a reality, but we found that this was only a matter of externals and that most of the people were too enjoined in parish politics to respond to the message of the Gospel of Jesus Christ. The Sunday morning congregation numbered about forty, and it did not increase whilst we were there, as the whole neighbourhood knew of the unhappiness within the church.

We worked hard amongst the youth of the parish, as at Todmorden, and even began a Church Youth Club, in conjunction with the Local Authority. We took the young people away for a Continental holiday, but none responded to the Gospel message, which Anne especially continued to embrace with her unflagging evangelical zeal. When Cliff College Trekkers came on a mission to Barnsley, she enthusiastically went along to support them. But I was too spiritually low to respond.

My job description seemed to be: Money Raiser for the Church Renovation Fund; Museum Curator for tours of the ancient building; Archives Researcher for Americans who wanted to trace their family trees; and Arbitrator of Peace to a divided congregation.

After two years, sickness struck the family again. The children, as well as myself, had recovered from the asthma of Todmorden; now I began to have a serious and debilitating infection in my throat, so that I could hardly speak. Acute sinusitis was diagnosed and an operation recommended. I was even in hospital over Christmas, leaving Anne to do all the work and the entertaining of relatives.

The operation was not successful, and the specialist came to the firm opinion that it was the fumes and dirt from slag heaps which were a constant irritant; he advised another move. So, after three years, but thankfully with the healing work well done in the parish, having absorbed all the hurt these dear people felt, we were once again signalling the Bishop for another parish.

This time the Bishop of Wakefield came up with a part of the diocese set on the top of a hill with large areas of beautiful moorland, the Shibden Valley, all around. It was the Church of St Matthew, Northowram, a middle-class suburb of Halifax. The church had been well served over a number of years by the Reverend Tony Wharton and his wife Marjorie.

We found that the life of this church was mainly based upon the principles of Christian Stewardship, which promoted the commitment of Time, Talents and Money. There had been a lot of good work done amongst young women, and there was also a fine musical tradition in the parish.

At that time there were no vestments worn, and Morning Service alternated between Holy Communion and Morning Prayer. Uniformed youth organisations were very strong, especially the Scouts.

The vicarage was a good building, amply large enough for our family and all seemed set for a valuable and fruitful ministry. I recovered some, if not all, of my evangelical zeal. Anne was as zealous for winning souls as ever, singing hymns and choruses in her devotions and having her faith firmly rooted in the Bible. She had never lost her straightforward faith and spiritual enthusiasm for a moment.

We soon felt, however, that we had hit a spiritual brick wall in our endeavours to further the Kingdom of God in the area. There were some sincere and devout Christians who had given themselves to the Lord as a basis for Christian Stewardship, but the rest looked upon the church as mainly a social institution and a centre for local secular activity. A sign of this was the popularity of the Northowram Church Players, a thriving drama group.

The frustration we felt was typified by the fact that when we tried to put on a Prayer Meeting and Bible Study at the vicarage, only five people attended, whilst when we had a Cheese and Wine Party, you just couldn't get near the place for cars and people. The most enthusiastically attended event at the church was the Annual Church Gala Day, when the Sunday School Queen was crowned; and by far the most successful event of our ministry was a Model Railway Exhibition!

I tried hard again with the youth, constructing a new Centre on the vast church premises, whilst Anne endeavoured to get her spirituality across as Enrolling Member of the Mothers' Union, a position which, in the natural, she never wanted to hold.

Events came to a head when Billy Graham was holding a Mission in England and there were to be relays of the meetings at Leeds, which was not too far away. Anne tried very hard to persuade the women of the Mothers Union to hire a coach to go to a meeting, hoping for a spiritual breakthrough in the parish. One of the leaders looked her straight in the eye and gave her reply:

"We shall not be going!" she exploded. "We are Anglicans, not Methodists. Anglicans we are and Anglicans we remain!"

Anne was devastated by this rebuff, which seemed to place her evangelistic outlook in her known Methodist background and was not a spirituality in the Anglican tradition. This middle-aged lady seemed to be speaking the mind and outlook of the whole church. The prospect of a visit to a Billy Graham Relay was abandoned. We both, but especially Anne, felt extremely frustrated.

I was, in fact, going through a crisis. I had now been a Methodist in Brighouse, a Curate in Todmorden and a Vicar of two parishes, without seeing any church growth or, even more important, any real extension of the Kingdom of God. "Was this," I was asking, "what I was called to do to serve the Lord after my conversion?" Something vital was missing! Something was sadly wrong!

During my time, firstly at Todmorden, then at Barnsley and lastly at Northowram, I had had experience of teaching in schools and colleges of further education. At Northowram I had actually had the experience of teaching Religious Education itself to the very keen pupils of Claire Hall Secondary School, and I found it very fulfilling. Was this the way the Lord was leading for the future? I wondered.

I decided that I was seemingly 'no good' as a parson, not really seeing any fruit for my ministry; whereas there were real indications of a response from the children and young people at school. Anne, too, had become increasingly unhappy, especially amongst the ladies at Northowram, as they had not responded to her evangelistic lead and only seemed to want a socially minded leader in their Vicar's wife.

We prayed and decided together that I should go into full time work in Christian Education. So after only two years at Northowram, I, a somewhat disillusioned minister of the Gospel, applied for the post of Head of Religious Education at Passmores Comprehensive School in Harlow, Essex, and was given the post.

We moved there into our own home in a neighbourhood named Deer Park in August 1967. I also took a post as a part-time Assistant Curate at St Paul's Town Centre Church. Anne did some nursing as a Marie Curie nurse, assisting terminal cancer patients so that families could rest at night.

The faithfulness of the Lord in building His Kingdom,

however, can be seen in a remarkable sequel to our ministry at Northowram. It seems that our ministry did influence one person at least, into an act of deep commitment to Jesus. A young married woman named Jean Hoggard did become very much spiritually alive. Even while we were there she had felt the call to full-time service and had begun a course of training. After a time as a lady worker in another parish in Halifax, she returned to minister at Northowram.

Years later in 1988 we received a letter from her asking us to go back and take some special services in the parish. We went to minister there over a weekend and found the parish, including people about whom we had once despaired, vitally alive in the Holy Spirit. The large church was packed and filled with the sounds of high praise to Jesus. We laid hands on many for the healing of body, mind, and spirit. The following year the Church Council unanimously asked us to go back and minister at another weekend for Spiritual Renewal. The Glory of the Lord again came down upon the gatherings. The church at St Matthew's, Northowram, is now in a very different spiritual dimension, and a great deal is the result of the testimony of one woman who has been faithful to her calling and uninhibited in sharing her experience of the Holy Spirit. Jean is now a woman priest in a nearby parish.

Chapter 8
"Receive the Baptism in the Holy Spirit"

When I am sharing my testimony with Christian congregations these days, I often say that I was a far worse teacher even than I was a parson. In fact, there came the time at Harlow when I felt a complete failure. Of course I had the knowledge from which to teach well. My two main problems, however, were the fact that it seemed Religious Education was regarded as the Cinderella subject at my comprehensive school, and also that I felt unable to maintain discipline in the classroom.

Certainly the children and young people were, in the main, very resentful at being compelled by law to open their Bibles and study the subject, especially as the majority of the children came from backgrounds where there was no interest in religion in any form. They seemed to regard their compulsory R.E. lesson as a time for relaxation and non-attention, all at the expense of the teacher.

Morning 'Assemblies' were little better, even when conducted by other members of the staff. The sight of youths lounging around, often with their hands in their pockets, some chewing sweets or gum, whilst pretending to sing hymns like "Praise my soul the King of Heaven", filled me with horror. I regarded it almost as blasphemy. It certainly was not the spontaneous utterance of adoring, thankful hearts, which is the essence of worship as seen from my point of view. I became more and more convinced that both compulsory worship and compulsory Religious Education were a mistake in secular schools.

The problems I faced at school were not helped by the way in which even '0' level or G.C.E. Religious Education was set as a direct alternative to other subjects, as the pupils who elected to take it were those who were academically incapable of doing anything else, and who, save for a few exceptions, didn't want to take the subject seriously anyway. It was difficult to try to teach such unwilling young people against this background. It is not surprising that I spent three quarters of my time trying, often unsuccessfully, to keep order, and only one quarter teaching the few pupils who wanted to know about the great events of the Bible and Christian history. I devised all manner of ways of presenting the subject and many different teaching techniques, but I became more and more strained and, in the end, it became a real effort to go to work.

The situation was alleviated to some degree by my post as Curate at St Paul's, the Harlow Town Centre Church. I worked under a Vicar, the Reverend Donald Knight, who had brought a genuinely evangelical emphasis to the church from its found-ation. The other Curates were also very keen Christian young men, and the people really wanted to hear the Gospel and to receive deep Biblical teaching. We had delightful fellowship with some of the church folk; but it was hard for me to play even a junior role in the parish, especially after days of exhausting work and stress at school. It was also unfortunate that the parish malcontents tried to fasten on to us to air their views. However, generally life was happy for us as Christians in the town centre church.

By the time we had moved into Harlow we had become a family of six. Anne's father had passed away into the full life of the Kingdom of Heaven whilst we were at Silkstone. Rachael, our third daughter, had been born there, and Philip, our only son, had been born at Northowram. We had, therefore, a young family and Anne worked hard in the home. She even managed some secular employment in order to help us meet the mortgage repayments on our three-bedroomed house. She made our home unfailingly comfortable and attractive, and it was always very clean and tidy, a place of welcome and warmth. She tried as far as possible, also to play her part in church life, especially supporting me, and she was very happy with the spirituality of the church.

It was whilst we were in Harlow, however, that Anne's only brother, George, was found to be seriously ill with cancer, and it was this crisis in her family which proved to be the beginning of a new, wonderful discovery of spiritual truth and experience for us both.

"Whatever can we do to help George?" was Anne's continual question to me. "I know we can pray for him, but isn't there anything else we can do?"

"We can hopefully use our influence to get him into a Hospice once his illness has advanced to that degree," I replied on one occasion. But this didn't satisfy Anne.

By what we can only regard as God's good providence, we met an Anglican Vicar named John Tyndale-Biscoe, who was showing a Christian film at the parish church, and we invited him and his wife Margie to our home for supper. We instantly liked this couple, who seemed to radiate the peace of Jesus. Anne began to share her problem about George's critical illness with John.

"I know a Pentecostal Church at Welwyn Garden City which is visited by an evangelist named Peter Scothern," volunteered John. "He certainly has a gift of Divine healing, because the Lord used him to heal my neck of severe arthritis."

Anne immediately became interested, and after they had gone home she told me that she was certainly going to go to this church in search of God's healing for her dear brother.

"I shall certainly not be coming with you!" I exclaimed, somewhat angrily. "I don't believe Divine healing is God's gift to the Church today and in any case, from my knowledge of Pentecostals, they are theologically unsound, emotionally unstable, and generally a people to be avoided."

I then reminded Anne of the time we had, on our

honeymoon in Scarborough, actually gone to a Pentecostal Church and witnessed a highly emotional scene when a group of worshippers, led by the Pastor, had tried to 'pump' the Holy Spirit into a young boy through getting him frantically to take deep breaths. He had in the end become hysterical.

And then there was the occasion, I reminded her, when we had been present at a healing service at Bridge Street Elim Pentecostal Church whilst we were students in Leeds. Subsequently we had met a woman who had not been healed of diabetes; she had almost gone into a coma because she had not wanted to inject herself any more with insulin.

"No," I emphasised. "You won't find me dead in a Pentecostal Church. If you want to go, then you'll have to go by yourself."

Anne, however, was determined to try any means spiritually possible to save her brother's life. She made enquiries, and one evening set off on the thirty-mile journey to the Hyde Valley Pentecostal Church at Welwyn Garden City, on an evening when Peter Scothern was to conduct a meeting there. She also took Rebecca, the elder of our twin daughters, to keep her company, as she had expressed a desire to go, too. I stayed at home to look after the other children.

It was after midnight when Anne and Rebecca arrived home from the meeting, and even then they had been brought home to Harlow by some Christians in their car.

"What happened?" I asked, having struggled for at least two hours to avoid becoming too anxious. "Was there some kind of after-meeting, or did you have coffee somewhere?"

"No dear," she replied in her usual soft, sweet tones, "the meeting actually lasted three hours!"

She was very excited about what she had seen, and described the service in graphic detail. I was impressed by her enthusiasm and especially her account of having seen a woman who had been paralysed for fourteen years get out of her wheelchair, in the Name of Jesus, and walk around the church. She had also seen several people converted to Christ in what had obviously been a very inspiring and joyous, and yet orderly meeting.

"I spoke to Peter Scothern about George," Anne went on, "and I told him how serious his condition is. He lives in the Nottingham area, like George, but he didn't make any promises about visiting him. But he did promise to pray for him. There was even a lady there who gave a prophecy. She said that George would be miraculously healed! Isn't that wonderful!"

And so Anne was filled with new hope. I said that I would take her to the next meeting she wished to attend at Welwyn Garden City.

It was about two weeks later that we were able to go to the Pentecostal Church for what turned out to be a baptismal service. I decided to go incognito, not wearing my clerical collar, but with an open mind, to see if I was as impressed as Anne. I was, in fact, feeling spiritually desperate, following what I felt to be my failure as a Christian minister and my intense difficulties as a school teacher.

We arrived together and sat in the back row. We were both thrilled with the meeting. There was a deep, spontaneous reality about the worship, especially the singing of 'spiritual songs' or 'choruses' which truly expressed the joy of the Christian life and confidence of faith. We heard 'speaking in tongues', prophecy and other spiritual gifts, and were especially impressed with the 'singing in the Spirit', wherein the congregation of about sixty people sang in tongues, in an unknown language peculiar to each worshipper, with a tune they had never learnt; yet all was beautiful harmony.

We also saw some people being ministered to for healing, and four people went forward to give their lives to Jesus Christ, something I hadn't seen for many years. We were very impressed. At the end of the service I went to speak with the

Pastor, Lewis Adcock.

"Where do you get this spiritual power from?" I enquired with sincere and earnest eagerness.

"From heaven," replied the Pastor. He then went on to ask, "Who are you? I don't think we've ever met before?"

I told him my name and explained that I was an Anglican clergyman.

"Are you born again?" enquired the Pastor.

"I've just told you that I'm an Anglican clergyman," I retorted somewhat impatiently.

Lewis Adcock didn't seem particularly impressed, but when I briefly recounted my Christian experience he was convinced that I really knew the Lord.

"You have offered ministry here tonight," I continued, "for everything except that which I'm desperately seeking -- what Peter Scothern preached about -- the 'baptism in the Holy Spirit.'"

"Would you like to receive?" asked the warm-hearted Pastor.

"I certainly would!" I replied fervently. "What do I have to do?"

"Simply come into our small vestry and I will bring in the elders to pray for you," was the promising reply.

I went into the vestry and sat down on what was, in fact, a wet chair, still dripping from the last baptismal occupant. The three elders and the Pastor began, together, to lay their hands on my head and to pray with great fervency that the Lord Jesus, from His throne in heaven, would send down the Holy Spirit on His believing servant. They pressed hard and prayed loudly. I was somewhat confused, as they repeatedly prayed, "Receive the baptism of the Holy Spirit."

"You seem to get your neck broken to receive this blessing," I thought, and the idea that all their enthusiasm was because they didn't get an Anglican clergyman every week floated through my mind! I just didn't know what to do to respond in any way to what was happening, but I prayed with all my heart that the prayers of these lovable, open-hearted, sincere and dedicated men might be answered. Eventually, after fifteen minutes they finished praying and seemingly, nothing had happened to revolutionise my spiritual life.

"How do you feel?" enquired the Pastor.

"Wet!" was all I could honestly reply.

"We are sure that God has visited you and filled you with His Holy Spirit," declared an enthusiastic Lewis Adcock. "You will see the difference."

As we journeyed home in the car, we were an excited couple, feeling that we had, together this time, discovered a new dimension to the Christian faith and determined to return to the Pentecostal Church as frequently as possible. We had received nothing but a warm reception and as much help as Pastor and people could give us.

Anne, at this stage, didn't feel in as much spiritual need as myself and hadn't received ministry. But she was eager to learn more about the power of the Holy Spirit. Her main concern was still for George.

During the following weeks I did find that something remarkable had happened in my Christian life as a result of the prayers which had been said over me. I had a continual desperate desire to pray and especially to praise the Lord, and I took every opportunity to get alone to commune with my Saviour. The Bible took on new significance and meaning as I avidly read its pages, and I seemed to have new eyes for the signs and wonders of the New Testament, the glory of the Lordship of Jesus and the Person and work of the Holy Spirit.

Members of St Paul's Church, Harlow, remarked that there was a new, positive, authoritative note and clarity in my preaching, and I found new freedom in speaking enthusiastically to the children at school about the power of Jesus to change lives and heal sick bodies. I still wasn't satisfied, however, because I felt that I had only partially received what the Lord had in store for me. I felt thirsty for more and thought that I would, if commanded by the Lord, start to drink the River Thames dry if it would bring further blessing!

It was, eventually, at 9.0 pm on 10th May 1969 that my deep longings were met by the grace of the Lord Jesus Christ. Anne had gone out for the evening and had left me to look after the four children. I prayed a prayer of faith over them: "Go to sleep, in the Name of Jesus," I said, and almost immediately they went into deep and peaceful sleep.

"Now I have two hours, at least, for prayer," I thought, and I went downstairs, got down on my knees and began to praise the Lord aloud. I did this for the space of at least an hour, with the Person of the Lord Jesus Christ, seated high on the throne of the universe, as the object of my praise. I began to sing choruses I had learnt at the Pentecostal Church over and over again, and eventually I found that I ran out of words in English with which to express my love for Jesus. Suddenly, my tongue seemed to go completely wild and almost out of control, tending to beat on the roof of my mouth; then sounds began to come from my throat, eventually shaping into words that I did not recognise or understand. It seemed also that there was a huge hole in the ceiling of the room and that the house no longer had a roof. I lifted up my eyes and saw a glorious throne surrounded by a dazzling white light. I heard angels singing beautiful songs, the meaning of which, like my own words, I didn't recognise, except I knew that I was joining with them in singing songs of praise to Jesus. It went on and on. I felt my heart was bursting and that I was no longer on the earth.

"I ought to have left a note for Anne: -- Gone to heaven, will be back later," was the only earthly thought that entered my mind.

Eventually, I did come down to earth, as it were, and I

knew that I had experienced what Peter Scothern had called my personal Pentecost. I had been filled with the Holy Spirit. I reconsecrated my life immediately to the Lord's service. My prayer included the words: "Use me O Lord, just as you will! Send me wherever you want me to go!" The Lord was very soon to answer this prayer in many wonderful ways.

In the meantime, however, we received news which was a severe blow to our new-found faith; George's cancer had spread throughout his body and he now had a secondary growth in his lungs. He had become very seriously ill and had been admitted to hospital. We sought all the spiritual help for him that we could, including a visit to him by a devout Pentecostal elder in order to administer the laying on of hands and 'anointing with oil' which the Bible prescribes in the Letter [Epistle] of James.

Despite all this ministry and prayer George became increasingly ill and suffered excruciating pain. As a result of all the spiritual attention he had received, however, he had become a sincere Christian, playing tapes of spiritual choruses and messages while he lay helpless in bed. His faith continued to be strong as he believed for his healing, and he even booked a holiday in Cornwall in anticipation of being miraculously healed. We hung almost desperately on to the prophecy which had been given to Anne in the Pentecostal Church, that he would be healed by the intervention of God. It was not to be, however. George died at home, having in faith discharged himself from hospital by ambulance despite being in a critical condition. This was in June 1969, a month after I had been baptised in the Holy Spirit.

From a human point of view, the devastation caused by George's death and the failure of that misguided, albeit sincere prophecy, should have left us so disillusioned that we should have turned our back on the validity of healing ministry. However, all had not by any means been lost, because George had died in the faith of our Lord Jesus Christ which, humanly speaking, would not have happened if Anne had not sought

Divine healing for him, with all the accompanying prayer and ministry. Also the spiritual truths into which we had now come, especially in relation to new life in the Holy Spirit, were too real to be denied. We don't know why Anne's only brother's life was taken from him at the early age of thirty-two, despite all the promises to which we had clung, but we do know that George was and is with Jesus in His heavenly Kingdom. I conducted what was an inspiring and joyous funeral service and we determined to go on with Jesus into whatever work He would now lead us.

Chapter 9

"Will you teach us about the gifts of the Holy Spirit?"

I had, without doubt, received into my Christian life the power of the Holy Spirit which had been promised by Jesus to His followers. The question I was asking now was, "What am I going to do with this experience? Had Jesus blessed me," I asked myself, "solely so that I could have a personal, closer relationship with God, or was there a further reason for this spiritual endowment?"

As I studied the Bible, I became convinced that this power was in fact given by the Lord to His people so that they could be more effective in serving Him; that they might be His 'witnesses'. It became clear to me that the power was given by the Lord primarily to His Church; it was, to use the phrase of Michael Harper, "Power for the Body of Christ".

I began to feel the call of God back to ministry specifically within the Church, especially in a parish, and I therefore wrote to the Bishop of Chelmsford, Right Reverend John Tiarks, and asked if there was a possibility of returning to parochial ministry. The Bishop replied, suggesting that we had a look at the parish of St Paul, Hainault, actually on the outskirts of London, but also in the county of Essex. I telephoned the Churchwarden, Mr Will Tyrrell, and made an appointment for us to see the church and area.

When we arrived in the locality of Hainault we motored around for over two hours trying to find the church building; no one, it seemed, knew where it was! Eventually we were directed on to a very large housing estate which we later learned had been built after the war by London County Council in order to house returning servicemen.

The first thing we noticed was that there was not a private house in the area and that many of the council houses were of a prefabricated construction. Eventually we found the church building, down a narrow back street, hidden from view except for those who lived in close proximity. It was a fairly small building which looked, like the houses, to have been pre-fabricated.

It stood on waste land, with a new-looking, but relatively small church hall next to it; a tarmacadam area in the front of both buildings made parking available for about five cars. Despite the fact that the small wooden tower appeared to be broken down, it was obvious that someone cared for the place, because a small area of grass which also fronted the church building had been cut and a 'garden of rest' between the church and the hall was very well kept and festooned with roses.

"Hello there!" beamed Will Tyrrell, as he greeted us on the forecourt. "Would you like to see around the church?" He further introduced us to the other Churchwarden, Joe Dawson, who was, I learned, an elderly retired working man and who spoke like a Cockney when he made himself known.

The door was duly unlocked and our gaze swept around the unattractive interior. Old-fashioned gas fires were mounted on the walls, and electric wires protruded from the low ceiling. Will Tyrrell explained that a local electrician was slowly re-wiring the church, free of charge.

We went over to the organ and were told that it had been constructed out of a do-it-yourself kit and that several notes didn't actually play. The three vestries seemed to be full of old junk, but the place was obviously loved and kept clean. However, the whole building, which seated, we guessed, about one hundred and eighty people in second-hand pews, was desperately in need of renovation.

The church hall was little better than the church itself, and all the items used by the many organisations were stored in old wardrobes. Anne and I were singularly unimpressed. We studied the Service Register and discovered that, at most, about thirty-five people made their Communion at the main services.

When they saw the rather despondent look on our faces, the Churchwardens suggested that we should quickly move out of the church buildings and go to have a look at the vicarage, the nature of which Anne especially was most interested to see.

If the church had been a disappointment, the vicarage was a mini-disaster. It was very small, especially for a family of six, and had obviously been built just after the war in 1945, when severe restrictions still applied to the building of new houses. So there was only one tiny bathroom, two small double and two small single bedrooms. The kitchen was also very small and bare. The decoration was in a dreadful state, as were the few carpets and, as with the church, the place was in need, in the interior at least, of complete renovation. Our hearts sank.

"If You want me to be used in revival," I murmured to the Lord, "what about Westminster Abbey or St Paul's Cathedral?"

"You can't ask me to come here!" Anne whispered to me, in the privacy of the bathroom.

"Isn't it all awful?" I replied.

We had both made up our minds that this wasn't the place for us. As we walked back towards our car the Churchwardens suggested that we might like to come back and meet with the Parochial Church Council before making up our minds about whether to accept the Bishop's invitation. We felt that nothing could be lost, and so agreed.

It was at this subsequent meeting that we began to understand something of the spirituality of these few dear Christian people.

"If you come here, will you lay hands on sick people?" asked Will Tyrrell.

I was absolutely astonished by the question, coming from an Anglican Churchwarden in 1970.

"We've reached a point in our Bible study where we've come across the gifts of the Holy Spirit, such as 'speaking in tongues' and 'prophecy'," ventured Joe Dawson. "If you come here will you be able to teach us about the gifts of the Holy Spirit?"

It was at this moment that I realised that God was indeed calling us to work for the extension of His Kingdom at St Paul's, Hainault. Anne, however, had yet to be convinced. She was still having problems with the nature of the area, the smallness and condition of the vicarage and the subsequent well-being of the family.

Later, at home, she expressed to me once again her serious doubts about the whole venture.

"I can't possibly go, myself. And I can't take the children to Hainault!" she affirmed.

So strong was Anne's determination not to go to Hainault that I actually wrote to the Bishop and declined his invitation to go to be the Vicar of the parish.

Anne, however, had always been very sensitive to the voice of God, and it was about four o'clock in the morning a few days later that she suddenly sat bolt upright in bed, awakening me by the force of the change of position.

"Trevor!" she said excitedly. "I was half awake when the Lord spoke to me and told me that we had to go to Hainault. Now I desperately want to go. I will be very disappointed if we don't go. In fact we *must* go!" Anne has only ever wanted to go God's way.

We were excited together as we praised the Lord for so clearly making His will known to us both. The next day I wrote again to the Bishop and stated in my letter that we were so sure we had to go to Hainault that we would 'make do' with the problems of the vicarage.

Consequently I left Passmores Comprehensive School in Harlow, we sold our house and decided to take the whole family for a month to Butlin's Holiday Camp at Skegness, where I was to do a temporary Chaplaincy before we moved to Hainault.

The month at Skegness proved to be, in fact, more than a holiday for the family. I was full of the Holy Spirit and ministered in such a way that several members of the staff at the camp, including Ray, the Children's Entertainer, committed themselves to the Lord and were filled with the Holy Spirit.

My small office became a place for late night Bible Studies and prayer meetings, the like of which Butlin's had never seen before.

Anne, as a good wife and mother, also had her mind on the home we were to move into at Hainault, however, and left Butlin's early in order to see that the home was ready for when we moved in. When I arrived there with the children, what I saw took my breath away. The church had had central heating installed, and Anne had followed this by having the home completely re-carpeted, curtained and decorated, all in a very short space of time. The furniture had arrived from Harlow and the previously unattractive home had been turned into a miniature palace. We were all thrilled because, through Anne's gifts and endeavours, we knew we would settle most happily into St Paul's vicarage. Anne has always felt that, within our means, a Christian's home should glorify the Lord -- and our new home certainly did that.

I was inducted as Vicar in September 1970, to the strains of the hymn "To God be the glory, great things He has done". We were ready for a new beginning.

*   *   *   *   *

I soon began to introduce changes into the church's programme. One which was to prove very important was a new Church Fellowship which met every Tuesday evening. There was, however, at this early stage, nothing particularly different in character about these meetings from any fellowship groups in other churches.

The dozen people who came were mainly middle aged or elderly. Church services went on very much as before but with the introduction of a Guest Service and a weekly Family Service. In these, again, nothing particularly remarkable happened. The turning point came when, as we studied the Scriptures together, I shared fully with the people my deepest spiritual experiences, especially that of my new endowment of the Holy Spirit. I talked of Peter Scothern and his ministry and of all I had received at Hyde Valley Pentecostal Church under the ministry of Pastor Lewis Adcock.

We then began a short Divine Healing Service once a month after the Tuesday evening Fellowship meeting. About a dozen people would gather in the church to pray for the sick, in a loose liturgical framework as some knelt at the Communion rail and whispered to me their own needs or the need of some relative or friend. I would then lay my hands upon their heads and pray extempore according to each request, but I felt that there was no real power in the meeting. They were in an 'Anglican' ethos -- very different from the free, spontaneous, joyous evangelistic type services at Hyde Valley Pentecostal Church.

Ten folk however, having had their curiosity aroused by our description of the meetings, went there with us to a service conducted by Lewis Adcock. These people just didn't know what to expect. The service was well under way when Pastor Adcock made what, to me, was a startling announcement. As usual, he asked sick people to go forward for prayer, and then he said:

"We are pleased that tonight we have here the Reverend Trevor Dearing and some of his people, and I will ask him if he will now come and lay hands upon the sick."

I was thrown into confusion. True, I had ministered to

people the Anglican way at my monthly services, but to minister at a Pentecostal meeting, with people standing, whilst the congregation praised the Lord in song, was quite different. Further, in my Theological College training they had taught me how to bury the dead, but not how to heal the sick; certainly not this way. I slowly went up to Lewis Adcock and whispered:

"I don't know how to do it; not your way."

His reply was comforting: "All you need to do," he said quietly, "is to put your hands on their heads and pray for them in tongues, your new spiritual language."

Hesitatingly I went up to the first person, closed my eyes, stretched out my hands, put them on her head and prayed in 'spiritual language'. Suddenly I felt her seemingly disappear. I opened my eyes and to my astonishment, saw her lying flat out on the floor.

"Well, she wasn't very well anyway," I thought and went on to the next person. Immediately I laid my hands on his head he keeled over backwards. In a few minutes all the sick people lay on the floor. They had not been hurt at all as they fell, however. It was a spiritual happening which I, at that time, did not understand. The Pastor was very excited.

"You have the anointing for healing, given to you by the Lord!" he exclaimed.

I had felt the power of God go through me in a remarkable way as I had abandoned myself to Jesus and ministered in this atmosphere of hearty singing, expectant prayer and powerful faith. A young lady from our church received healing for a nervous breakdown and later testified to a local newspaper: "Prayer saved my fight for sanity". Now I knew that God would use me in this way, and immediately determined that our services at St Paul's would change.

There was, however, yet another significant event in that particular service. As I was ministering, I felt led to say, "There is a person here tonight who has no reality of Christ in her life, even though she has been going to church for years. I am going to ask that person to come forward and accept Christ."

To my surprise, Jean, a member of St Paul's almost since it was built, stepped forward.

Another member said to her, "It can't be you. You've been a Church Member all your life."

Jean retorted, "I know my own heart."

It was a moving moment as Scots-born Jean, a member of my Parochial Church Council, accepted Christ as her personal Saviour and Lord. It was just as exciting for me, as I had been used by the Holy Spirit to win my first soul for His Kingdom after many years. Jean was, in fact, to be the first of thousands.

PART TWO

The truth in action --

*The visitation of the Holy Spirit
to
St Paul's, Hainault 1970 - 1975*

Chapter 10
You shall receive power

In those early days at St Paul's, Hainault, I realised that I had arrived in more ways than one. I was the leader of a body, albeit a small one, of sincere believers who made the sacrament of Holy Communion their central and most important act of worship. I soon moved the altar forward, put the rails around it, and celebrated the Eucharist every Sunday morning from the ancient westward position in a quiet atmosphere of profound devotion.

The fact that vestments were not worn did not bother me, as I regarded them as a fringe issue. I emphasised to my people the grace God conveyed through the bread and wine of Communion and the water of Holy Baptism. I continued to make my Liturgical Confession of sins in the presence of a priest. The Catholic emphasis of my faith was fulfilled.

A nucleus of the people of St Paul's also turned out to be students of the Bible. They wanted to be taught Bible theology. I was not a fundamentalist in the way I had met it at Cliff College before studying for my Degree, but I had a profound belief that the Bible was deeply inspired and that its truths should be expounded. I was still certainly an evangelist believing in the power of the Bible's message to change lives. The people welcomed this approach. All this had been deeply intensified through my experience of Baptism in the Holy Spirit which changed my insight into Biblical truth, from black and white, as it were, to colour and three dimensions. This experience brought me a close awareness of the Presence of Jesus and a new expectancy of what He would say and do. I had a new freedom in speaking to people about Jesus, and a new authority in preaching. I had entered into the supernatural gifts of the Holy

Spirit (1 Corinthians Chapter 12) and the whole supernatural realm had become real to me.

After a few months I was to learn that not only Pentecostals, but ministers of the major denominations, including the Church of England, had embraced this deep teaching about the Holy Spirit, as I read of Reverend Dennis Bennett's experience in America at the Church of St Luke's, Seattle; and as I met up with Reverend Michael Harper and the Fountain Trust. It seemed that what I had received was in no way isolated, but part of a new, real move of the Holy Spirit in His Church. This was being called the 'Charismatic Movement', because of its emphasis on the 'Charismata' -- Greek for 'spiritual gifts'. In my own view, however, I could accept no labels. I had entered fully into Truth, Evangelical, Catholic and Pentecostal.

It was in February 1971, when I eventually felt that the Church at Hainault had been well prepared, that I asked the evangelist Peter Scothern to conduct an evangelistic healing service for our people. We had been very impressed with what we had seen of his ministry on his visits to Hyde Valley Pentecostal Church. We felt that he was the man who could bring a real spiritual breakthrough at St Paul's.

Although it was widely publicised, however, the evening was, in some ways, relatively uneventful. Of the eighty people who came, only eight rather nervously received the laying-on of hands from Peter Scothern for healing, and there were no visible miracles. Nine people, however, made what were to be lasting decisions to follow Christ.

After the drama of the previous Scothern meetings, we found this to be a rather uninspiring occasion, falling far short of what we had hoped for; that was until I went into the vestry, where a small group of church members had gathered to receive what Scothern described as a "deeper Christian life through a more dynamic experience of the Holy Spirit," -- in other words, the Baptism of the Holy Spirit. About a dozen seekers were there as, one by one, Peter Scothern laid his hands on them asking God to have His way completely in their souls. The small vestry was filled with the sound of praise!

The next day the telephone hardly stopped ringing with the testimonies of those who had been blessed. I answered the phone.

"Vicar," said Min Tyrrell, the Churchwarden's wife, "I've had a strange experience. I found that in the night I woke up and wanted to shout and sing for joy. This morning I found strange words coming from my lips which I didn't understand. Can you tell me what's happened to me?"

"You've been baptised in the Holy Spirit, just like the believers in the Acts of the Apostles," was my joyful reply.

Then Freda, the Church Treasurer's wife phoned.

"Vicar!" she exclaimed. "I was hanging out the washing on the line this morning and suddenly I had to rush indoors to praise the Lord in tongues!" She went on to explain that she had come to the meeting hopeful of receiving healing for her chronically bad back, and had misunderstood Peter Scothern's directions. She hadn't realised that those going into the vestry were not seeking healing, but rather a new experience of the Holy Spirit. She had got into the wrong queue! But, nevertheless, God had richly blessed her.

My heart leapt with excitement as member after member called to recount similar experiences. Soon our little flock began to talk freely about Christ, saw new truths in their Bibles, entered into a new enthusiasm in every aspect of Christian life and also into a new realm in worship and in prayer. Their joy in the Lord was infectious!

We invited Peter Scothern back a month later for yet another meeting, and this time the church was packed to capacity, mainly through the testimony of those who had found new spiritual life through his previous visit. Peter continued to visit St Paul's on a regular basis for four years, and every time he came there was a rich anointing of the Holy Spirit upon the meeting. St Paul's, under God, was very indebted to his contribution.

In the meantime, however, my own ministry was developing rapidly under the inspiration of the Holy Spirit. After I had entered into a new dynamic in healing ministry through Lewis Adcock's invitation to me to minister at Hyde Valley, I decided to start 'Power, Praise and Healing' Services of my own at St Paul's. At first these were held once a month, but in due course, because of the ever-increasing demand, they replaced the Church Fellowship on a Tuesday evening and became a weekly occasion.

I abandoned the set form of healing around the Holy Table for a ministry of extempore prayer, related to the specific needs of each individual. My prayers, however, were uttered with new authority, conviction and power, amidst an atmosphere of expectancy expressed in praise and worship. I always preached about some aspect of the essentials of the Christian faith as part of the service before ministering to the sick, and many people responded to be counselled for conversion to Christ. Anne was, at this stage, in charge of the counselling ministry which was deep, decent and in order in our adjacent church hall.

The church began to be packed with people every Tuesday evening. We bought two hundred chairs, which were placed in the aisles, in the chancel and sanctuary area behind where I was preaching and leading the service. People sat on the floor and on window sills in order to get a place in the building. Queues of people began to form outside the church as early as four o'clock in the afternoon, consisting of people who wanted to be sure they would get in. Crowds of people came from all over Essex and London; some from as far away as America and even Singapore.

The work of the church was featured in every national newspaper in England and even in foreign languages, as journalists came from overseas. Radio and eventually television reports covered the phenomenal events which began to take place in the small, back-street, parish church at Hainault.

Typical was the report by Stuart Hyslop of the Southend Evening Echo, who wrote sympathetically and with enthusiasm about the Healing Meetings:

"Everything about the meeting at St Paul's is relaxed, most people came casually dressed. There are people at the door to give them a friendly welcome. No questions are asked. Some people have been before, many will come from different Churches, different religions or have no religion at all.

"There is no ritual, few trappings. Mr Dearing, apart from his clerical collar, dresses as casually as most of the congregation in light coloured, flared trousers and a jersey. Music comes from a small group and from the Church organ. It is catchy, unrestrained and all about joy and putting your trust and love in Jesus. Everyone sings cheerfully -- people leap from their seats, waving their hands. There are cries of 'Hallelujah'. Mr Dearing walks about in front of the Church, sometimes he talks to the congregation and joins in singing. Then Mr Dearing and the congregation pray and he bursts out speaking in tongues. Immediately Mr Dearing stops speaking another member of the congregation bursts out with a fluent English interpretation.

"When Mr Dearing makes his call for the sick to come forward, about thirty respond, some in callipers and crutches and one in a wheelchair. Throughout the meeting there is a sense of expectancy. There is always the possibility that someone may have a miracle cure, as has happened so often before, or Mr Dearing may have to struggle with a demon. Another thing everyone looks forward to is his message. He gives it off the cuff, walking up and down the centre aisle."

Another press account was by the Methodist Minister, the Reverend Albert Cornah. In an article in the Methodist Recorder he wrote:

"Over 400 people crowded pews, aisles and porch. Gospel hymns and choruses rang out. Cries of joy and praise punctuated the prayers. A simple but scholarly exposition of a Bible passage was made, then a ministry of blessing offered with the laying-on-of-hands for healing and Baptism in the Holy Spirit.

"A trickle of folk, then a flood, came forward, and those ministering seemed submerged beneath the numbers seeking. One, two, three hours passed and no one wanted to go home. Today around 450 meet each Tuesday and you couldn't squeeze any more in. To get in you go early, to get a seat, very early."

So the meetings went on, every Tuesday evening from 1971 until we left St Paul's, Hainault, in December 1975. Every week it was the same story; crowds flocking into the church; spontaneous praise and worship often lasting as long as an hour; an evangelistic message based upon the Scriptures for about forty minutes; a call for people to come forward to be counselled about new spiritual birth, and a prolonged personal ministry for everyone who was sick; deliverance, often amidst the screams and shouts of demonic forces possessing human lives; personal ministry for Baptism in the Holy Spirit; testimonies or letters read, usually by Anne, from those who had been healed or whose lives had been changed; a time of quiet but authoritative prayer for the absent sick, usually timed for 10.00 pm so that needy people could tune into prayer across the miles. Other ministers, especially Bill Worboys, Jim Rattenbury and John Tyndale-Biscoe often shared this ministry.

All finished with a time of ecstatic joy and worship of a

living, triumphant Lord who had, as always, demonstrated His Presence and His power in the midst of His people. God visited St Paul's Hainault, its Vicar and his wife, by His sovereign will, with true Holy Spirit revival. All this was a fulfilment of Jesus' promise: "You shall receive power when the Holy Spirit comes upon you."

Chapter 11
To you and to your children

When the Holy Spirit began to move at Hainault, Anne was not sure that she really liked what was going on. She had come to love the Sacraments and other Prayer Book worship of the Church of England, but found the new meetings of uninhibited joy, clapping, hand-raising and much more free expression of emotion, disturbing. She felt that it was all neither respectable nor dignified. It was all right in the Pentecostal Church, but in the Church of England she expected a different approach. She was delighted to see the people giving their hearts to Jesus in real conversion experiences, but was alarmed at people falling down under the power of the Holy Spirit when hands were laid upon them.

"It will never happen to me!" she exclaimed on numerous occasions, "I always keep control of my emotions."

Anne therefore became increasingly unhappy as events unfolded at St Paul's. On the surface she looked all right to most people who attended the Tuesday meetings. She always greeted people with a smile and she was in charge of all the counselling of the enquirers for salvation. She was also constantly at the sacraments, spoke well of the blessing that people were receiving in the name of Jesus, and after all, she was married to the Vicar who was the leader of what was going on.

Despite appearances, however, Anne was becoming depressed. What was happening at St Paul's had shaken her spiritual security which she had found in the traditional evangelical and Anglican ways of thinking and doing things. She felt spiritually dried up after all our years of uneventful Christian ministry; she wanted to be blessed by the Lord, but not in the way He seemed to be blessing people at our gatherings.

It was at one of the Tuesday meetings in 1973 that she made up her mind to be real with God, in the presence of His people, about her deep spiritual needs. She decided, she says, to come from behind all her past tradition, her 'respectable' Anglicanism, the fact that she was the Vicar's wife and a church leader; from behind all the appearance of "looking good" and seek God's blessing in His way. At the end of the ministry time, when everyone else with needs had gone forward, she felt she would go forward too and seek the baptism of the Holy Spirit. The devil, she says, whispered in her ear:

"Don't you go forward; you look all right, and everyone thinks you are all right. Don't make a spectacle of yourself, stay where you are!"

"Get thee behind me Satan!" she answered firmly, "I know my needs."

She came forward to receive the laying-on of hands. It was the Reverend John Tyndale-Biscoe, now one of the assisting clergy, who ministered to her. She stood for a few minutes on her feet, and then to her surprise, found herself gently falling backwards into the arms of a steward, who laid her on the floor.

"I felt such peace," she said afterwards, "and I knew I was soaking up the Holy Spirit like a dry sponge soaks up water."

After a little while Anne rose to her feet and returned to her seat with a deep sense of peace almost overwhelming her. That evening, after the service, she returned to the vicarage full of joy. We went to bed but she couldn't sleep. She sat up reading her Bible with new spiritual eyes, insight and excitement. She sang aloud choruses she had learnt at Cliff College years ago.

"Darling, aren't you going to go to sleep?" I exclaimed at three in the morning; "I have an early engagement tomorrow."

"I don't know what's happened to me!" she replied excitedly. "I just can't stop singing."

"You've been baptised in the Holy Spirit," I explained as

I switched off the light.

Anne didn't initially speak in tongues or sing-in-the-Spirit, but she found that the Lord imparted other lovely spiritual gifts to her quickened soul and spirit. She immediately received a penetrating gift of 'discernment', and then prophecy and the ability to interpret other people's tongues, as well as a wonderful wisdom in the things of God. Her spiritual life would never be the same again as she moved, as I had done, into a new dimension of spiritual experience and ministry.

Our daughter Rebecca also soon entered into blessing, even as a young child. She experienced this at a meeting I was taking at Stratford, East London. She explains:

"I was bubbling over with praise and thanksgiving as I worshipped my heavenly Father. The power of the Holy Spirit fell upon me and I found myself lying on the floor speaking in a new tongue. Since that time my life has been changed. I had always found it difficult to tell people about Jesus, but since then it's a joy, for I love speaking about my Saviour. Praying has since been an inspiration to me, for I enjoy talking to the Lord. Before my baptism in the Spirit, prayer was a burden. The baptism in the Holy Spirit has indeed released me in my spiritual life and has filled me with an everlasting peace and joy."

Rebecca soon began to minister in a deep and profound gift of prophecy which the Lord has used to speak through her ever since.

Our youngest daughter Rachael's life was gloriously transformed as she gave her heart to the Lord at a mission for children at our nearby Evangelical Church and now, years afterward, lives for Jesus. Ruth, Rebecca's twin, has always been walking with Jesus since Hainault days.

Philip had a quaint experience. At the age of seven he was once crayoning in a colouring book at a meeting. Seemingly he was unconcerned at all that was happening around him, though he had given his heart to the Lord a year before. However, as

I began to minister to seekers after the baptism in the Holy Spirit he murmured to Anne that he too was going forward to ask Jesus for this blessing, as he wanted to speak in tongues. He stood there amongst the adults as I kept passing him by.

"What about me?" he asked.

The co-evangelist, Jim Rattenbury, prayed over him and he went down to the floor speaking in a new language. He then went back to his crayoning.

"Did you receive the gift?" asked Anne.

"Of course I did," was his reply. "Jesus did it." Then he added, "I won't use the gift at school though, because the Headmaster wouldn't understand."

Philip was also the subject of a healing miracle. One Tuesday evening as we were beginning our meeting a message was brought into the church that he had gone over the handlebars of his cycle, falling flat on his face. His face was flowing with blood, we were told, and several parts were badly gashed. Anne rushed him to the hospital where he was detained over night. We prayed for him at our meeting, and the next morning the hospital doctor could not believe what he saw; for Philip's face was perfect, as if nothing had happened!

Through all these wonderful blessings, the Lord deepened further the profound love which has always been the essence of our family life. Our beautiful marriage relationship was given an even deeper dimension and our family life was centred constantly in the reality of the Love of God. The Lord was preparing the children also for the willing but deep sacrifices they would make for the Lord's sake as we began missioning together. What the apostle Peter had said to the crowds on the day of Pentecost was fulfilled, "The promise is to you and to your children."

Chapter 12

Signs and wonders shall follow
the preaching of the Word

Miracles of healing were a regular manifestation of the power of the Holy Spirit at St Paul's. Testimony after testimony was given at the Tuesday meetings and Sunday services of God's power to heal the sick in mind and body. Accounts of some of the healings actually appeared in newspapers after the reporters had interviewed some of those who had been healed. One of the most remarkable articles appeared in the News of the World on January 20, 1974 under the headline: 'Astonishing world of Trevor the Vicar'. It had the joint byline of John Lisner and Franklyn Wood and began:

"A group of Vicars will meet this week to debate the extraordinary healing claims of the trendy Rev. Trevor Dearing, whose followers say that he has already been barred from working his 'miracles' in some Churches.

"Last night, the 40 year old healer's Bishop, the Rt. Rev. John Trillo, told me: 'I am all for Trevor Dearing's ministry. It would be a funny business if everybody in the Church was alike. He has a particular gift. People are uplifted by him. If people believe they've been healed, that is good enough for me.'

"Of reports that the Vicar had been barred from some Churches, the Bishop said, 'He has not been barred by me. A lot of traditional Church people feel uncomfortable about this sort of preaching, but I wish I had a few more Trevor Dearings.'"

The News of the World article went on:

"Mr Dearing usually treats people by placing his hands on

77

their head. 'I don't ask for them to get better,' he said, 'I tell them to get better. I don't lay claim to healing in every case. It's not me anyway. It is God who cures them through me.'"

The paper, which has one of the largest circulations in the world, decided to investigate the case of Yvonne Perry, a young woman in her early twenties, whose doctors had told her mother that she would need a miracle in order to live. Yvonne was being treated for a rare and serious blood disease. A slight cut would have meant that she would have bled to death. She was in danger of internal haemorrhaging.

Mrs Perry told the News of the World: "I went to see Mr Dearing and we prayed together. He told me, 'Your daughter is healed. Don't pray so hard now, something is on the way.'"

She added that doctors were astonished when they next saw Yvonne. She was cured.

Another case featured was that of Mrs Christine Brown, who for eleven years had wanted a baby. For the first two years Christine and her husband John had not bothered too much, but later, when nothing happened, they went for tests. They kept going for treatment for seven years. She told the paper: "Then I began to believe that adoption was the only way, so I went to the Church thinking that the Vicar's recommendation would be useful. Mr Dearing laid his hands on me. I fell back and fainted. I felt a great heat when he touched me. Two months later I was pregnant. Little Melanie is living proof of a miracle."

A very thorough investigation of my healing ministry at St Paul's was carried out by the mass circulation American newspaper the National Enquirer. The article, written by Donald T McLachlan, had this headline: "Doctors and Cured Patients acclaim Amazing Healing Powers of the Mod Minister."

It read: "Afflicted people are flocking to be healed by a Mod Minister near London whose powers are acclaimed by hundreds -- including medical doctors whose patients he has helped.

"'The Rev. Trevor Dearing is a most unusual man and I believe he has the gift of healing,' says Dr David Frampton.

"He spoke of seeing what the long-haired Minister did for his patient Joyce Cowans.

"Mrs Cowans, 54, of Ingatestone, Essex, England said: 'A terrible auto accident left me paralysed from the neck down, my spinal and vocal cords were damaged and my bladder injured. They told me to wear a drainage tube for the rest of my life. But I've made a wonderful recovery and no longer need it.'

"Dr Frampton confirmed, 'There was a dramatic change in her condition after she saw Rev. Dearing. She can now walk unaided and her internal injuries -- which medical treatment could not further help -- are now cured. There is no doubt in my mind that the Rev. Dearing was responsible for her recovery.'

"A patient of a London doctor, Eleanor Blunt, 65, had a heart attack. The doctor reported, 'I prescribed digitalis to strengthen her heartbeat. Patients with this condition seldom recover completely.

"'On October 10 last year Miss Blunt went to see Rev. Dearing and was cured. I can see no other way she could have been cured other than by divine healing.'"

Another newspaper, the Romford Reporter, featured the moving case of baby Joanne. Their story read:

"A young mother cuddled her baby daughter as she stood before a crowded congregation and told them about little Joanne's remarkable recovery from the brink of death.

"Mrs Wendy Doherty, 33, said: 'Joanne is now much better and we are looking to God to heal her completely.' Six months ago the 16 month old Joanne was dangerously ill with bone marrow disease. Her body was not producing anti-bodies and she was open to infection. But now her parents believe their prayers are being answered after taking Joanne to see Mr Dearing. 'She no longer has to have any medicine but she still has injections.'

"Mrs Doherty and her husband Ronald decided to visit Mr Dearing on the advice of their family doctor, who is a friend of the Reverend.

"'We were sceptical but now we cannot deny there has been an incredible improvement in her condition,'" said Mrs Doherty of Blackmore Road, Brentwood. 'After taking Joanne to see Rev. Dearing several times during the past four weeks, the baby was tested at the Children's Hospital, Great Ormond Street, London.'

"On Tuesday, as Mr Dearing laid-on-hands on Joanne he said, 'We must pray to God for a miracle. Lord let thy healing hands be upon Joanne now and let your healing grace flood her bones.'"

Another baby that we remember being remarkably healed was the child of Salvation Army Officer parents. The baby had been born blind. They brought her to St Paul's on a Tuesday evening and I laid my hands on the baby's eyes.

"Let there be sight, Lord," I prayed. I went on: "Jesus, who healed the eyes of the blind Bartimaeus, heal this child's eyes now."

On the following Thursday the baby had another appointment with Moorfield's Eye Hospital which was caring for her. The parents telephoned the vicarage excitedly on Thursday afternoon.

"There's been a miracle!" they exclaimed. "Irises which were non-existent in our baby's eyes have actually appeared and grown and the glaucoma has subsided. They say she can see!"

The last contact we had with that family was when the parents sent us a photograph of their daughter some years later, actually riding a bicycle down the road.

There was a murmur of surprise on another occasion at a Tuesday meeting when an attractive young mother was carried into the church on a foam bed. The slow, sad procession proceeded up the aisle to the front of the church, where the lovely-looking woman lay there helpless like the paralytic who was let in through the roof during Jesus' ministry. Her pretty face was contorted in agony from the constant shocking pains from her damaged spine. Her sister-in-law had brought her all the way from Sudbury, Suffolk, in a desperate bid to free her from her anguish.

The congregation joined me in believing prayer as I asked the Great Healer, Jesus Christ, to touch her spine, heal her, and take away all pain. I commanded her to rise in the Name of Jesus. God heard that prayer and the young woman was able to get to her feet, a new person. She was weeping tears of joy, as were most of the congregation. Her sister-in-law wrote to us later stating:

"From that moment she has been completely and absolutely fit. She experienced a sensation which she described as warm 'pins and needles' but no more pain and she is now able to sit and move easily; in fact she is now so well that only three days after coming to your meeting she travelled 400 miles in one day, sitting all the time. She now has her small baby back home, after his being with us for fourteen weeks. When I took him back a couple of days ago, she had been doing all her housework and looked completely well and happy."

God also healed many emotionally ill people at St Paul's. One was Marcia, who gave her testimony on the television programme, 'Doctor Jesus'. She had been suffering from a deep depression that got darker every day. She was healed in a ministry one Tuesday evening which, she said, lasted half a minute.

Another was Carol, who suffered intense depression, needing treatment in a psychiatric hospital following the breakdown of her marriage. After being healed by the Lord she actually became a nurse in a psychiatric hospital and won the 'Nurse of the Year' award. She is now married to an Elim Pentecostal Pastor.

Pat, a full-faced London infants school teacher was another brought to the church suffering from intense depression. It started after the death of her father, with whom she lived. When she came for ministry her neurosis was so severe that she was unable to communicate. She sat like a rag doll with her head between her knees. She had been in this condition for several days, and her doctor had agreed that Christian friends should bring her to Hainault. I began to pray for her and as I did so God showed me clearly the details of her problems. I began to tell her that Jesus was making this known to me, that God knew her needs and was answering them. Promise after promise came to her from the Lord. In the end I commanded her to come out of her 'prison-house' and break the chains with which Satan had imprisoned her. The next morning, instead of being taken to a psychiatric hospital, she was back at school teaching her class of energetic children.

Another young wife, Sue, from Wanstead, tells her own story: "I had never regarded myself as a depressive, quite the opposite, until I was expecting our second child. My first pregnancy had been wonderful, but my second was dogged by bad health and mental stress from the outset. James was born at home three weeks before we moved into a house which needed more than a lick of paint to make it habitable. My husband, bless him, was working to get the worst jobs done and, as Jamie was two weeks late, my mother, who had offered to look after me, was on holiday.

"Nine days later my child had an accident. I was losing ground. I imagined my depression would lift when we moved but it was quite the reverse. I became easy prey to fits of uncontrollable temper. I would shout and scream and throw things.

The child whom I dearly loved was my whipping boy, and after that I would sit and sob in depression. I loathed what I'd become; every night I vowed tomorrow would see me patient and loving, yet every tomorrow was a nightmare of hysterical temper and self-condemnation. Then I tore a pillowcase in half during one of my bouts and that night I begged the Lord to help me.

"A friend of mine had read of the St Paul's meetings and, knowing that I was seeking the Lord, asked me to go with her. I went expecting something, I don't know what, but not to give my life to Christ. I returned home with a soggy handkerchief and a splitting headache. That night I had virtually no sleep. Next morning my head was still pounding and I felt drained, but when I looked into the garden I realised I was no longer alone -- the Lord was with me. Jesus had taken away living death and made me a gift of life and wonderful peace and joy in His love.

"That's it, the beginning I mean, for the Lord has blessed myself and my family, time and time again, in more ways than my appreciation can grasp. Praise Him! He does not barter His love as so many of us do, but gives it undeservedly and without reservation to all who seek Him."

Each week, at our Tuesday meetings, we looked out on a sea of expectant faces. Like that of Ruth, a small, dumpy former Salvation Army Officer and nurse in her late sixties. She had served as a medical missionary in India, but serious illness forced her to leave full-time service. When she came to St Paul's she firmly believed that the Lord could help her.

It was during the sermon, she later testified, that she first felt healing from Jesus flowing into her body, bringing blood back to her limbs. She had been suffering from hardening of the arteries, resulting in extremely poor blood circulation, so that for months she had had hardly any feeling in her hands or feet. Her fingers and toes had turned black, and at times during the night she suffered excruciating pain, which not even eight hot water bottles resting on her feet and hands could relieve. Often she paced the floor in sheer agony, not knowing how to cope with the pain.

Ruth also suffered a severe thrombosis in one leg. She had felt that her days of health and service for Christ were over, until at that meeting she felt a tingling going through her limbs. When she later received the laying-on of hands, she went back to her seat and, to her delight, found that her hands had returned to their normal colour, her legs and feet had new life. She felt waves of health sweeping through her, and has never experienced any return of her symptoms.

Dan Chapman arrived at St Paul's with a white stick, and as he tapped his way down the aisle he hoped that God could do something for his near-blindness. He arrived at the service having had three heart attacks and operations for cataracts on both eyes. He says:

"I first came to St Paul's after my last eye operation. I could see so little that I had to walk with a white stick. Within three months of starting to go to St Paul's I could see television and read, my doctor says I have got on remarkably well."

And to add to Dan's joy, his wife was also healed. Before she first came to Hainault she was paralysed, and was told she would have to wear a surgical collar for the rest of her life. "But Mr Dearing took it off and she has never had to wear it again," he says.

Margaret had been blind in one eye from birth. She received sight instantly in that eye after prayer.

Another sight healing concerned an older woman who came forward for proxy healing on behalf of a sick absent friend. When she returned to her pew she was startled to discover that she herself had received sight in a blind eye.

'Woman' magazine featured another of these healings. Their account read:

"A 39 year old mother of three in Romford, Essex had both

eyes permanently damaged after two major brain haemorrhages six years ago. A Specialist from Moorfield's Eye Hospital told her that she would never see properly again.

"'I was a doubting Thomas to begin with,' she said. 'I was in terrible pain and desperate. I needed to be killed or cured. I didn't want hands laid on me, and I didn't want to faint and make a fool of myself. I don't like demonstrations.

"'So I just closed my eyes and had a most marvellous experience. I've never known anything like it before or since. I felt I was being carried upwards by four angels and then brought back. There was total peace and no pain.'

"She fell to the floor and later, as she went back to her seat said that she recognised faces that had only been blurs before. Now she can see clearly with her left eye, though there is only a speck of light in her right eye. Hospital tests have shown the difference in her sight before and after, but she says the doctors can offer no explanation."

Deafness as well as blindness was healed by the Lord at St Paul's. One of the most moving cases was that of a country Vicar in Essex, who loved to listen to classical music, but because of his deafness was deprived of this pleasure. I prayed for him and he wrote afterwards to say he could now hear even the faintest sounds of individual instruments in the orchestras.

Epilepsy is a terrible affliction. It is a Cinderella amongst sicknesses. Sufferers go through untold mental agony, not knowing when they will have their next attack, and many are unemployable for this reason. One such epileptic was Trevor from Ilford who, after being healed for over three years, could not find employment because employers just couldn't believe he was healed after being so ill.

He told his story to the Southend Echo:

"I first started having epileptic fits when I was 12, and was

having three a day when I came to St Paul's. I didn't have
any faith until I experienced the atmosphere and the way of
worship here. It was a wonderful experience and relieved me
of anxiety about my condition. I believe faith has completely
stopped my attacks."

We also had healing from cancer, that most dreaded of
diseases. Again the 'Woman' featured the story:

"Mavis of Ilford, Essex, is a 53 year old woman with two
grown up children. Two years ago she was told she had
malignant cancer of the cervix -- the neck of the womb.

"'I was desperate,' she said. 'My mother had died of cancer
only five months previously and I knew life to be so
precious.' Mavis, a Salvation Army member, went to a
healing service at Hainault.

"'When the Vicar laid hands on me in the Name of Jesus,
I fell backwards under the force that burned right through
me,' she says.

"After six weeks of radium treatment the doctors told her
there was no trace of cancer left. She believes Divine healing
and hospital treatment worked together in the healing process."

Children received healing ministry regularly at Hainault as
well as adults, and remarkable healings took place as they trusted
in Jesus.

One such was Melany, a little girl with a hole in the heart,
who was found to have been healed after ministry.

We had a special time at exactly 10.00 pm every Tuesday
at St Paul's. This was our 'Prayer Link Up', when we prayed
for the absent sick who were asked to 'tune-in' with us in prayer
in all parts of the British Isles at that time. It was a time of quiet
and intense concentration as request after request for prayer was
read out and we believed for healing across the miles.

There were many great miracles which took place as a

result of this time. One such was when a young married mother with two children wrote saying:

"I am writing to tell you of the wonderful progress my mother has made since having been prayed for at your 10 o'clock Link Up. She stood up by herself at that very moment. She is now back home and the nurses are amazed that she could stand up and walk after such a serious illness resulting from a fall."

Another emotional answer to prayer during the Link Up took place only hours before Anne's late step-father Len was due to have his right leg amputated. Len, a retired bus driver, had found himself crippled up with pain from blood clots in both legs. One cleared up with hospital treatment but the other remained blocked, and gangrene was setting in. On the Tuesday night before the operation was due the next morning, we prayed for him at St Paul's at our 10 o'clock Link Up, and the blood immediately began flowing into his right foot.

Next morning the surgeon came to see Len and had to blink when he saw the doomed right foot flowing bright pink.

"This is remarkable," he said as he scratched his head. "Do you believe in miracles, Mr Ford?" he asked.

"I do!" replied Len.

"Well, as long as you live, remember you've got a miracle right foot!"

'Words of Knowledge', another gift of the Holy Spirit, also flowed at St. Paul's, especially through my lips as I would describe, through Divine inspiration, the exact needs of someone present in the meeting and promise that God would heal, as He always did.

A southern midwife now retired, Mollie Cerver, wrote about such an occasion. "A midwife friend of mine omitted to mention to you the ulcers in her mouth. Two weeks ago she had fifteen teeth out, dentures put in and had suffered much pain from ulcers. The Lord gave you a Word of Knowledge about someone on the left of the church with a painful mouth that He had healed. This morning -- praise the Lord -- no ulcers."

Another instance of this remarkable ministry came to light at a Convention I was conducting. A mother put a baby in my arms, proudly announcing: "There is your perfect baby."

"You see," she said, "I was one of a congregation of five hundred people at your meeting. I was terribly worried because I had contracted German Measles soon after pregnancy and was faced with the possibility of having an abortion. I was in a terrible dilemma. Suddenly, as if speaking directly to me, you stated that you had a revelation from God about a problem of pregnancy and German Measles.

"You said the promise of God was that if the woman would keep the child it would be born perfect. Here it is!"

We had dozens of people who told us later about instantaneous, glorious, direct healing by Jesus through such revelations about the definite touch in sufferers' lives at our meetings at St Paul's.

Jesus commissioned His Church to "Preach the Gospel, heal the sick and cast out demons." The Bible says that signs and wonders would follow the preaching of the Word. This was proved to be true at St Paul's. We have seen how the sick were healed at St Paul's, Hainault. We will now turn to the casting out of evil spirits to His glory and extension of His Kingdom.

Chapter 13
In the Name of Jesus

There was a time in my life when I did not believe in the devil or any other personal powers of evil. I felt that man alone was ultimately responsible for all the evil in the world, and that to lay any blame on a so-called 'devil' was merely to seek a scapegoat. These beliefs were intensified by the liberal theological education I received at Wesley College. I regarded the Biblical and even the New Testament teaching about the reality of evil powers as merely a belief of the times, a sort of first-century superstition that needed demythologising in order to make sense for modern scientific man. I had studied psychology in depth as part of one of my Degrees and felt that all bizarre emotional feelings and excessive behaviour could now be explained in psychological terms. I held these views more or less firmly until I was baptised in the Holy Spirit in 1969.

The experience of being immersed in the Holy Spirit immediately gave me more faith in the Bible's teaching. I now had a new, inspired insight into the teaching and meaning of the Holy Scriptures. It just came to me as a gift from God. I began to see that Jesus must indeed be seen to be absolutely accurate in His teaching about ultimate spiritual realities. Jesus, I saw, certainly taught the reality of the devil and his kingdom of evil; He definitely cast evil spirits out of the hearts and lives of tormented and sick men and women, and they were made completely whole. He also gave His disciples "authority over all the works of the devil." All this teaching, however, still seemed rather remote until I was confronted with Olive Allen. She became my first case of 'deliverance' or 'exorcism' ministry.

It was at a time, early in our ministry, when the Tuesday meetings were still small, with only about twenty people attending. Someone introduced me to Olive, but she was hardly friendly: "I've had enough of your ministries," she told me curtly.

The third time she came to church she spotted a stack of Bibles near the door and felt drawn to them. I noticed her from the pulpit as she began to tear a Bible into shreds, and went up to her to see what was going on.

She turned on me with glassy eyes and said in a weird-sounding voice: "I am witchcraft and I have come to destroy you before you destroy many of me."

I just didn't know what to do; I had never experienced anything like this before.

Later Olive came to see me, and she explained that she had been a witch for over twelve years. She was desperately trying to get free and urgently needed help, but I was still very new to this sort of thought and language, and didn't really understand what I was up against.

She came to the church again, this time with her husband Fred, and once more fell into some sort of trance. I didn't know what to do, so I set about anointing her with oil as prescribed in the Letter of James (Chapter 5 v 14) for the healing of the sick. This was the worst thing I could have done, because she became very violent and began to fight me. In the end the Holy Spirit Himself came to the rescue. He came upon me and I heard myself saying: "You spirit of witchcraft, come out of her in the Name of Jesus! I command you to leave her at once!" I shouted.

Suddenly she let out a great ear-piercing scream and fell to the floor. After a few moments she recovered and cried out excitedly, "It's gone! It's gone! It's left me!"

Then I had to minister reassurance to the congregation, because this kind of thing didn't usually happen in services in the Church of England!

This was not, however, the end of the matter, because evil spirits kept on invading Olive. On one occasion in her home a demon came out of her, but it entered her hapless dog. The poor thing lay on its back kicking frantically with its legs in the air. I prayed over it and learned that I had to cast evil spirits into 'the pit' to await the judgement of Christ.

Then Olive was experiencing terrible pain in her back, and her husband asked me to go and pray for her again. I laid my hands on her while she was actually blacked out. She came round and began to move her legs. Another spirit causing a spinal problem like that recorded in Luke's Gospel (Luke 13 vv 10 - 16) had now gone and Olive was healed of an affliction she had had for twelve years.

The problems, however, went on. She asked Fred to buy her a Bible, but three weeks later it was in shreds. She had torn it to pieces in one of her satanic trances. Again I had to minister deliverance from evil spirits and again she was set free. All this time she was receiving counselling, and her faith in the power of the Lord to keep her was growing. She began to trust in Him and asked Him most sincerely to come into her heart and be her Saviour.

The coven, however, where she had practised her witchcraft, heard that she was turning to the Lord, and one day a man called.

"Your group want you back," he said on the doorstep.

She told him she would not return, but he came back a few days later with the frightening threat:

"The coven has cursed you with the Curse of the Three Demons and you will die in six months," he said menacingly.

Olive was terrified, because the coven had used the curse on three different occasions while she was a member, and all three people had died.

"The Curse of the Three Demons lasts six months," she told me. "Firstly you are taken over by the demon of 'fear', then by the demon of 'despair', then by the demon of 'death'."

Shortly afterwards, at a Tuesday meeting, she went into a

trance and almost strangled her husband. As he gurgled and gasped for breath I stopped her in the Name of the Lord and expelled the demon. Her hands relaxed from around Fred's neck and she sat down, not knowing what she had done. Three months later I exorcised the demons of 'fear' and 'despair'.

Soon after, the evil man returned again and told her the exact date of her death -- September 16th. This was a Sunday and she and her husband came to church. Olive had until the evening to live if the curse was to come true. I knew about it as she came forward for this last desperate battle. There was a mighty struggle as I cast the demon out. Olive was blaspheming and cursing Christ. I then commanded the demon of death to come out in the Name of Jesus.

Olive later told me that she suddenly got a terrific pain in her chest and went into a sea of blackness. Many thought she had died. But the demon yielded to the anointing of the Holy Spirit and the authority of the command: "Come out in the Name of Jesus." She was free, and became a wonderful Christian, testifying to the power of Jesus to deliver from all that Satan can put upon the children of men.

In all, over a period of twelve months, I had cast twelve demons out of her soul. I no longer needed convincing about the reality of the devil and his minions, demons and unclean spirits which could inhabit the human heart and cause the most terrible spiritual, emotional and physical problems and torments.

"I'm now a complete Christian. I have been filled with the power of the Holy Spirit and am very happy. I'm also free from pain and worries," was the glad testimony Olive continually uttered.

Olive was far from being the only case of deliverance ministry at St Paul's, Hainault, although she was indeed the first. Ever after the Lord seemed to send 'demonized' (the Biblical term for 'demon possessed') men, women and even young people to St Paul's for release from their bondage.

One such young person was Barbara, who stalked around the vestry like a wild animal.

"That man's too powerful for me!" she yelled, pointing at me. "I can't stand him! I hate him! What's in me hates him!"

The girl was tortured by Satan. She had dabbled in the occult and was now paying the price of her curiosity and illicit spiritual adventure. She began to lay hold of small items of furniture and smash them. She broke a mirror that hung on the vestry wall. There was a terrific struggle before the demon left her, in the Name of Jesus.

Another time, as I began preaching, a young man in his teens suddenly let out a howl like a werewolf and started running backwards and forwards across the back of the church. He had his teeth bared and would have bitten people if he could.

A shiver went through the congregation as stewards pounced and tried to grab him. He told us later that he had been having horrific nightmares, going into trances and having violent outbursts. He had once drawn a knife on a friend. He also felt something urging him to commit suicide.

I took control of the whole situation and addressed the spirits in the 'werewolf' who cried out from within him. I told them that their reign of terror had ended, then cast them out in the Name of Jesus. The young man fell to the floor and then, just as suddenly, a moment later sprang to his feet and shouted, "Praise the Lord for all He has done!" It was astonishing. We all rejoiced at the transformation.

Once I was even summoned to a local school after three frightened schoolboys had told their headmaster that they had all gone into trances whilst playing with a ouija board during their lunch time. One had brandished a knife on a schoolmate after being ordered to kill him by the "spirit of his dead grandfather". Following the incident the headmaster, a Christian, asked me to pray for the boys because they had all become violent. After prayer all the boys were gloriously delivered, one from a 'familiar' spirit which had used him as a medium during the session.

In our experience people who try to become mediums in Spiritualistic "Churches" often become possessed by evil spirits. One such was 'Mary', a widow who actually turned up at one of our Tuesday meetings.

"I'm having horrific visions and hideous manifestations since I've tried to become a medium," she told us. "I'm desperate to find an answer, can you please help me?"

So I prayed with her and she accepted Christ as her Saviour, then received the baptism in the Holy Spirit and was delivered from her hellish experiences. Afterwards I introduced her to another believer, and in due course I had the happy privilege of conducting their wedding ceremony. She was the first of many former 'spiritualists' who were converted to Christ after seeing the power of the Holy Spirit at St Paul's.

Often we had to break the power of curses which were deeply affecting people's lives. For instance, Marina, a heavily built West Indian woman, told us how she had reeled with terror as she had discovered a cockerel's head, with horrible protuberant eyes, staring up at her from the wooden dining-room table of her London home. For, at that moment, she knew that a voodoo curse had been put upon her and her family. The terror of that chilling curse made her shake uncontrollably with fear. Her eyes rolled and her face twitched, for she feared that soon she would be dead. She had to escape the spell. But how?

For two years she was tormented in horrible, indescribable ways, quite unable to cope with her job as a teacher of handicapped children.

Then the voodoo terrors began to grip her even tighter. There was no escape from the macabre curse, and the frightening hallucinations became worse. Fear often drove her to violence and once, under the power of the curse, she nearly throttled two Pentecostal Pastors who were trying to exorcise her. They were only saved when one of them struggled free from her grasp, grabbed a phone and dialled 999 for police help. The struggling Marina was taken off to a psychiatric hospital; but there the powerful woman was often uncontrollable and they couldn't help her.

Marina came along eventually to St Paul's for help. She had heard of the wonderful spiritual power that flowed through the church. I immediately discerned a voodoo curse and knew that I would need to call upon every spiritual resource I had to set her free. As I began to pray, Marina went for my throat. Stewards came dashing forward and did what they could to restrain her, but it was the power of Jesus that held those demonic forces at bay as I began to break the power of the curse which was sending Marina insane.

For ten horrifying minutes the battle raged, and eventually the sweat poured down her ebony face as the evil spirit left her.

You couldn't believe the change that came over her. She began to grin, beaming out the real love which was in her heart. She was completely transformed by Jesus, the great deliverer, but she remembered nothing of the deadly struggle through which she had gone to be released. Marina is now a wonderfully committed Christian who has done splendid work for Jesus.

Sometimes in my ministry I had to cast out demons which were affecting people sexually. I once had to 'exorcise' a very attractive twenty-eight year old woman who, at the time, appeared in a very short mini-skirt and a scant blouse. She had an intense sexual problem.

I suspected that she had a demon when she got out of the doctor's car -- he had brought her to me for help. But she declared loudly that she would not go near me because I was "too powerful". We eventually got her into the church. There was no one else in the building at the time. The young woman ran out of the church into the toilets and Anne had to go to fetch her out. When eventually we began to pray she went into a trance and started rolling under the pews crying out, "I'm a demon of seduction!"

She had, it seemed, had a problem in that she just couldn't stop seducing men and having sexual intercourse with them at all times of the day. She was happily married but was driven to this intense sexual activity. Psychiatrists might have classified her as a nymphomaniac. Praise the Lord -- she was immediately and completely set free to be a happy woman, in control of her own sexual life through one ministry in our church.

A big circulation Sunday newspaper, the People, sent a reporter to attend a Tuesday meeting at St Paul's, who photographed a woman being delivered from what turned out to be another problem with sexual overtones. The paper explained that the woman, Jean aged 46, lived with her husband and two sons in South London. She had become tortured by bloody visions of death. They changed her from a happy housewife to a frightened, desperate woman. She heard voices encouraging her to do violent acts quite out of character. For example, a man's voice, with an Asian accent, commanded her to smash a portrait of herself which hung on her bedroom wall. She sought help unsuccessfully from doctors and psychiatrists. Eventually, in despair, she turned to a so-called spirit-healer.

His instructions were startling. He said she must have sexual intercourse with him. The spirits, he said, were commanding that she must bear his child. Jean later found that this man had been involved in a devil-worshipping cult.

At last she turned to the church. At the exorcism service the congregation sang and prayed as she retched and cried out at the altar rails.

"Mr Dearing," stated the paper, "Vicar of St Paul's and one of the Church of England's exorcism specialists, commanded the evil spirits to leave in the Name of Jesus Christ. The crisis passed and Jean is at peace again."

Another exorcism was dramatically caught by television

cameras which had come to record the ministry of our church. It was that of Jane, who was an alcoholic and had been involved in the occult. It began with the spirit crying out through her as she lay prostrate on the floor:

"Jesus is dead, I saw Him die."

"He is not dead, He's alive!" I shouted back.

"No He's not, He's dead! He's dead!" the spirit shouted back.

I began to speak in tongues and then commanded the spirit to leave. It was banished, and the next morning Jane's happy smiling photograph appeared in the Daily Express, as she testified to her complete deliverance. This ministry scene was shown on television across the nation in May 1975.

All this publicity brought needy people to St Paul's, Hainault, who were possessed by evil spirits. We sought, by God's grace, to help them all, and His Name was glorified as they were released and healed.

Chapter 14

If anyone is in Christ, he is a new creation.

Although we have seen so much of the Lord's power at work in healing and deliverance ministry, we remain convinced that the greatest miracle He performs is that of the transformation of human lives. We saw this at Hainault in the case of prostitutes who became Christians. Betty was such a person who was changed by the Lord from being an alcoholic prostitute into a devoted Christian mother. Another young woman in such a terribly fallen state of life to find the power of Jesus able to work a radical transformation, was Joan. She came to St Paul's, Hainault, looking for help. She too was an alcoholic who said she used men in order to get money for drink, and allowed them to use her for sexual gratification.

"What can you do to help me?" was her urgent question as she stood at the front of a crowded church. "I have had a baby, the only thing in the world that I really love, and today the health authorities took the little girl away from me, because they say I'm unfit to look after her."

Joan was shaking with emotion as she spoke. She looked haggard, twice the age that she actually was, with grey hair and furrowed brow. The way of life into which her alcoholism had driven her had exacted a terrible toll.

"I urge you to accept Jesus as your Saviour tonight and to put your complete trust in Him to save you," I said. "He is able to meet your every need."

Joan said that she would trust Jesus the best way she knew how, and was taken into the counselling room to be further prayed for and helped. Later that night she was taken into the home of one of the caring members of our congregation, who accepted her and sought to help her. After a few weeks Joan testified to the church that she knew that Jesus had delivered her from her alcoholism and saved her from a life of continuing prostitution. The health authorities saw a radical change in her and soon restored the little girl to her mother, to be looked after and brought up in the Christian faith. Joan eventually became an assistant matron in an Old People's Home and now is happily married to a fine Christian man who knows all about her past life. Jesus had worked a miracle of transformation in her.

Another addict whose life was completely transformed by Jesus at St Paul's, Hainault, was Jean. She was not addicted to alcohol but to drugs. She had many health problems and spiritual problems caused by the fact that, as a child, she had been offered to Satan on an altar by her parents. She was completely unable to get free from her addiction to drugs; she lied, cheated and stole in order to obtain money to acquire them. She had sought help at a Pentecostal Church, which sadly had rejected her without understanding the extent of her problem. At St Paul's she came to terms with her need, accepted Jesus, and she too was taken into a Christian home.

Like Joan, she is now a happy, responsible Christian wife and mother, living a life of service for the Lord.

Tony's problems were different from those of Joan and Jean; he was not an addict when he came to St Paul's; he was in fact a prisoner on the run from the police. He had escaped from Armley jail in Leeds and had fled to London, where the police were on the look-out for him. It was a cold and wet Tuesday evening when Tony saw the lights of the church shining brightly and heard the loud singing of praises to the Lord.

"The police will never look for me inside a church," he thought.

That evening I was preaching about the love of God for every individual in the world, no matter how sinful they had become. Jesus, I declared, had died for everyone. Tony had never heard this before, and certainly had never known that God really loved him, just as he was. The immeasurable love of God came home to his heart and, when the invitation was made, he went forward to accept Jesus as his Saviour and Lord. He was counselled by one of the Christian helpers and was determined to begin a new life. He immediately gave himself up to the police and was taken back to prison to complete his sentence.

There he gathered a group of fellow-prisoners around him to study the Bible. He led several of them to a personal knowledge of Jesus' saving work on the cross, one of whom is a Pentecostal Pastor today. Tony himself was released early because of his good behaviour. Friends from St Paul's kept in touch with him all the time, and eventually he became a city missionary in Leeds, working for a time for the Lord.

Another man who was transformed by Jesus at St Paul's was Bryan. He too had been in prison, but had completed his sentence by the time he came to one of the Tuesday Power, Praise and Healing Services. However, he was in a state of deep depression. It had been a degrading and humiliating experience to go to prison for fraud, because he was a 'respectable' middle-class man. His business had gone into liquidation and he was an undischarged bankrupt.

His first marriage had ended in divorce, and his second 'common law' marriage had also come to an end. He had no friends, money or home; in fact he had nothing left at all for which to live. He planned to commit suicide. However, at the service, he heard about the power of Jesus to transform every circumstance and situation of life, and he went forward for ministry. At last, he felt there was hope. His heart was filled with joy and peace, and a new life began for Bryan at that very time, as he trusted in the Lord.

He began a Christian ministry which brought blessing to thousands. All his circumstances were completely reversed and he is now married to a lovely, dependable Christian wife with whom he experiences complete happiness.

It was at a Tuesday meeting at St Paul's that John's life was also completely changed. He was a scientist who really didn't believe in God at all. He had serious doubts about the truth of the Bible. A young Christian man had however, gone to lodge with John and his wife, and he had spoken authoritatively to them about the Person of Jesus. John's wife Pauline was the first to give her life to the Lord under his influence, and she began attending all meetings at St Paul's. She told John about all the miracles of healing she was seeing and this aroused his curiosity, so he decided to come to a Tuesday meeting. As the appeal was given to accept Jesus, he later explained to me, he felt urged to go forward. As he stood in the line he said a prayer on these lines:

"Lord, if you are really there, if you really exist, then give me a real sign of your presence."

The next event that happened in the church was that everyone heard a tremendous crash and turned to see this man, John, lying on the floor in what seemed to be a doped stupor. No one had touched him but he had fallen like a chopped-down tree.

"OK Lord, I believe," John was heard to say.

He became a Christian in that moment and now is an Anglican clergyman working in the south of England. The power of the Lord is still at work today to transform lives. As St Paul wrote, "If anyone is in Christ, he is a new creation."

Chapter 15

Now you are the Body of Christ and members of each other

Miracles of healing and deliverance were not the only acts of God at St Paul's, Hainault. We always offered ministry for the baptism in the Holy Spirit, which had proved such a revolutionising blessing in the lives of both Anne and myself, and many hundreds received this life-giving empowering of the Christian experience. They nearly all immediately evidenced this by 'speaking in tongues'. Thus 'singing in the Spirit' was a regular expression of our praise and worship to God in our services.

The phenomenon of falling down under the power and influence of the Holy Spirit was also regularly but spontaneously experienced and witnessed in our meetings, and we had a whole body of trained 'catchers' standing behind people as they received the laying-on of hands. Sometimes, however, people fell spontaneously in the midst of the congregation, as a mighty 'anointing' fell upon them.

This is happening in a widespread way today in what is being called the 'Toronto Blessing' after the church in Canada where this new wave of the phenomenon recently began. All this was an outward evidence at St Paul's that God was actually present in our midst and results were being produced in a way which could be actually seen and heard.

The visitation of the Holy Spirit to St Paul's, Hainault, was not however, the result only of my own ministry. It was a sovereign act of God in response to a whole church which became open to His blessing as we waited upon Him. There were, for instance, always a group of people in a room adjoining the sanctuary, who were upholding in prayer all that was happening that evening; there was always in action a team of ministers who laid their hands on seekers. There were also about thirty trained counsellors who took people through a passageway into our church hall to explain the way of salvation, answer questions, deal with problems, give advice and further ministry if necessary. Anne was responsible for placing each counsellor with a particular enquirer and always prayed that the right 'match' would be made. And the come-back was that she was always guided by the Lord.

As our Tuesday evening gathering grew in the number of visitors and seekers from all over England, and indeed, from far corners of the world, we of the church itself soon became aware of another need. We realised that we had to meet together, as a church, in order to study, pray, and grow together. I therefore started, on a Thursday evening, what we called 'Growth Groups', meeting in members' homes throughout the area. It was to these groups that we referred new converts who wished to join our church. (Others were referred to churches in their own locality.) These met every week except for once in the month when we called all the groups together for what was known as the 'Body' meeting. It was at this meeting that God spoke to us in a corporate way.

The revelations and visions He gave us, as a church, were very illuminating. One such was of a huge oak tree whose branches spread out majestically in all directions. Its leaves swayed proudly in the breeze as admirers gazed in awe at its rugged beauty. But then a gale blew up and soon the mighty oak crashed to the ground. It had weak roots that couldn't really support its growth. This vision was a corporate one, shared and gradually enlarged by one member after another. Finally one person was given the interpretation, to the validity of which we all concurred. The tree was, in fact, our church, and its rapid growth was depicted in all the branches. There was nothing wrong with it growing quickly, but its roots were weak and shallow. God was calling us to put our roots more deeply down into His Being by prayer, meditation, and Bible study if the work of the Spirit was to endure.

Another corporate vision I vividly recall followed this dialogue:

"I've got a picture which I can't make sense of. It's a huge clod of earth-like clay."

"There's some hands around it," said someone else.

"Yes, the clod is being broken," added a third person.

"All the bits are falling from it!" exclaimed the first visionary, and, "as it crumbles I can see a beautiful shining jewel inside it."

"Yes, this jewel sparkles on every side," another added.

"Yes, but the ugly clod of earth needs to be broken before we can see the beauty inside it; a beauty that is already there but needs to be revealed," I explained.

We went on to see that God was 'breaking' us as a church and as individuals, by difficulties and trials, so that we could all reflect His beauty.

In response to this vision, we all sang the chorus, "Spirit of the living God, fall afresh on me. Break me, melt me, mould me, fill me. . . ."

We found such a freedom of expression at these meetings, such a warmth of love and power of faith, that every conceivable need was shared. People felt free to talk about their problems. For instance parents asked for advice and prayer from other members about the difficulties they were encountering in bringing up teenage children. Some spoke openly about temptations, trials, anxieties, stresses and fears. Also, as James urged us in his Letter, we confessed our faults and prayed for each other that we might be healed.

At one meeting a new member blurted out in great distress that she was addicted to amphetamines; at another a wife confessed that she felt she could no longer bear the strain of living with her unbelieving husband; at another a pensioner disclosed her desperate shortage of money. With these and many other needs, ministry and counselling surmounted the difficulties. We learned to "bear each others' burdens and so fulfil the law of Christ."

There were no social barriers at St Paul's, Hainault. People from diverse cultural, social and economic backgrounds, as well as members of all ages, were one in Christ. Members had also reached diverse spiritual levels. It had needed, however, this visitation of the Holy Spirit to be the necessary stimulus for fellowship on the lines of the early Church pattern. Believers shared deeply because they were moved deeply. As their commitment to Christ deepened, so did their commitment to each other.

A significant development for us was the revival of the New Testament expression of actually caring for each other in practical ways. Members in distress found their church friends to be of great help in constantly visiting them and by even helping to meet their financial needs. Mavis was one such. For many years she had suffered from acute agoraphobia. When her husband died, this nervous lady was left to care for two children, both of whom had real problems. She received regular help and support which enabled her to triumph over all her difficulties. Also I regularly handed out money from a special fund to help members who were unable to work through sickness or were unemployed, or to elderly couples who desperately needed a holiday.

Our concern, however, was not just for those inside the church. We were part of an ecumenical 'Community Care' scheme which had 'wardens' located in every area of that vast housing estate. These reported needs of which they had become aware where they lived. So we regularly visited local people who were known to be in need of care or other practical help. We also called regularly on scores of house-bound, aged and lonely people living in Hainault.

Hospitality was also readily and sincerely practised, as members welcomed strangers into their homes. Among those in such need of a home was Jean, an alcoholic who had just come out of a mental hospital, but was still unable to cope with the demands of life. It became obvious that she needed the continual fellowship, love, counselling and prayer of a Christian family. I made her need known at the Body meeting and immediately received an offer of a home with a church family. They also found her employment.

There was a meeting when I realised that another alcoholic who had been healed was in dire need of clothing. I made an announcement to this effect, and within an hour he had been given a suit and an overcoat by members who had spare clothing.

Ministers from other churches and denominations attended St Paul's whenever they could, and so we formed our own 'Christian Leaders' Fellowship' for those who wished to know more about ministering in the power of the Holy Spirit. One minister, the Rev. Albert Cornah, a Methodist, wrote: "I appreciate the privilege and unspeakable joy of being allowed to share in the ministry at St Paul's, in breaking new ground for me and helping remove certain inhibitions. Having been helped over the first hurdle, I shall be able to approach such a ministry here without many trepidations. I shall be grateful for your prayers as I approach a new circuit, that the work of the Spirit may prosper in my inexperienced hands. Many thanks for introducing me to the wonders of the charismatic ministry."

So the work spread to other churches in the London area as their ministers became involved with us.

Thus St Paul's, Hainault, had become a church which was dynamically changed for the better by a deep move of the Holy Spirit. I found this expression of Christianity really to work in a corporate and not only individualistic way. Religion became a reality. Everything was transformed: attitudes, meetings, conferences, services, music, clothes, and in time the building itself shone forth with a glorious but simple beauty. Those who stepped into it were conscious of being on "holy ground". We were all members who were united in our experience of Jesus in prayer and fellowship and ministry to all in need who came within our doors.

PART THREE

The truth at work
in all the world

Chapter 16

Fire from Heaven

In February 1975 Jim Rattenbury, a leader in our church who was recognised as a prophet, foretold in the Spirit, that the visitation of the Holy Spirit to St Paul's, Hainault, was coming to an end. He said that the central fire which was burning would die down; but that the sparks which had gone out from the fire would start spiritual blazes in many parts of England and, indeed, the world. Anne and I sensed that this was truly of God and began to seek the Lord about the nature of our future ministry.

We began to see the answer to our prayers for guidance in that St Paul's, Hainault, was not the only church where we had ministered since 1970. What the Lord was doing there had been "noised abroad" throughout Essex, London and the United Kingdom and we had received requests to take our ministry out from St Paul's to many other places. These requests had come from all denominations of Christians, from Pentecostal Churches to Roman Catholic.

When the church requesting a visit had been within two or three hours' journey from our home then we had taken the mini-bus St Paul's had purchased and had packed it with our people. They had given testimony about the wonderful transformation of their lives through the dynamic power of the Holy Spirit; they had told of their conversion, healing, deliverance from evil spirits or their baptism in the Holy Spirit. These accounts of the work of God had been very influential in persuading others in 'formal' church situations to seek similar blessings. Whole churches came alive with the power of the full Christian Gospel. In those days, we had to introduce congregations also to free, spontaneous, joyous worship and so had taken our own pianist or organist, Graham Dixon or David Freeman, together with our own song sheets, to these churches, and spent the first period of every meeting in teaching these Spirit-anointed songs to the people assembled for worship. These missions had begun at the Hyde Valley Pentecostal Church at the invitation of Pastor Lewis Adcock.

Following Jim Rattenbury's prophecy, in September 1975 Anne and I eventually went as a married couple, serving the Lord in partnership, to the island of Singapore. This was at the invitation of the then Bishop, Chu Ban It, who had himself not long been baptised in the Holy Spirit and had visited St Paul's, Hainault, to see for himself what was happening there. We visited several churches and schools in the Diocese and testified to the life-transforming power of the Holy Spirit. We took with us Graham Dixon, who was an inspired organist, to accompany free, spontaneous worship in the singing of the new songs which the Holy Spirit was giving to renewed churches.

At every meeting I preached the good news of Jesus Christ and invited listeners to accept Jesus as their own personal Saviour. We also ministered healing and the baptism in the Holy Spirit to hundreds of seekers. We held conferences and I gave lectures about ministering spiritual renewal to the clergy. The six weeks of mission reached a climax in meetings held in the Cathedral itself, which was filled to capacity on every occasion.

After this visit to Singapore, Canon Frank Lenax, vicar of the Cathedral, wrote in 'Network', the newspaper of the United Society for the Propagation of the Gospel:

"Christians old and new standing shoulder to shoulder in the Cathedral sanctuary and aisles sang in uninhibited joy -- some in tongues -- all with a new experience of the Spirit infilling with a new awareness of the living God and Father."

On the last night of the mission, a stranger wandering through the Cathedral grounds was drawn by the sound of singing and looked in through the west door. He later described what he saw: "The whole sanctuary was ablaze with fire. I closed my eyes in unbelief and opened them again. Flames of fire filled the whole east end . . ." It graphically described in visual form what was happening to those of us who were standing in the Lord's house.

Our visit to Singapore certainly helped forward the renewal work of the Holy Spirit in the Anglican churches there.

Especially clearly in our memory of our missions from St Paul's remains a visit to the Roman Catholic Cathedral of Westminster in the West End of London, for a special day of Spiritual Renewal. I had had serious theological doubts about whether Roman Catholics could be baptised in the Holy Spirit, as I had always regarded that particular Church as being in serious theological error. I even had an inner fear of the liturgy of the mass in general and of Roman Catholic priests and nuns in particular, in their celibate life and in the awe with which they were regarded by Roman Catholic believers. I had been very hesitant to accept the invitation. I was even more guarded when Anne and I arrived at the Cathedral to find the large hall in which we were to minister packed, not only with laity, but also with priests and nuns in cassocks and habits. "Could the Lord really bless here?" was my primary thought.

We were at once inspired however, with the worship, which was conducted to the accompaniment of guitars, and by the beautiful, reverential but fervent tone of the singing. At the appropriate time I was asked to speak to the assembled Catholics. I spoke about the power of the Holy Spirit which I had experienced in my own life and ministry and had been evidenced in our church. I urged the listeners to seek this blessing, saying that I would minister to seekers in a small, nearby room -- expecting only a few to respond to my invitation.

To my surprise the room became jam-packed, especially with priests and nuns, squashed together like sardines in a can.

I stood in the doorway and prayed inwardly: "If it is Your will, O Lord, send the Holy Spirit upon these people ."

Within the next few minutes there was such a visitation of the power of the Spirit that the seekers were not able to stand upon their feet. Priests crashed to the floor, lying over nuns who had also been prostrated by this mighty Divine anointing. Nearly everyone began to speak in tongues or sing in the Spirit in ways even beyond that which we had ever seen at St Paul's. Eventually, after what seemed a long time, the folk began to stand up on their feet uttering wonderful praises to God. There was a surge of Catholics around me, pressing in upon me, wanting me to lay my hands upon them in blessing.

"Bless me, bless me!" was their cry, urgently requesting the ministry of a Protestant vicar. I rapidly placed my hands upon one after another, and they all fell under the power of the Holy Spirit. We almost ran to escape the nuns who formed a corridor of seekers all the way from the hall to the car. Still as the engine started I had the window rolled down to reach out my hand to bless in the Holy Spirit one last petitioner.

It was a day to remember. I had now become convinced that God was no respecter of church or denomination, but that the Lord poured out His Holy Spirit on everyone who earnestly hungered and thirsted for Him. This was in fact, the first of several invitations to minister in Roman Catholic situations, where the power of the Holy Spirit was always seen to be at work. These visits included ministering to hundreds of Catholics at the first All Ireland Convention of the Full Gospel Businessmen's Fellowship in Dublin.

Throughout this time I had kept my Bishop, the Rev John Trillo of Chelmsford, informed about my missions outside St Paul's, Hainault, and had received nothing but encouragement and support from him. This liaison between myself and my superior culminated in 1975 after our six-week visit to Singapore. On our return the Bishop sent for me in order to discuss my future, about which we had been seeking the Lord. The Bishop explained to me that an Anglican vicar was really meant to be located in one church, a parish, and that the ever-increasing calls to minister in other places had put him in something of a dilemma.

"I believe," he said, "that you, Trevor, are called to serve the wider Church and must be released from ministry at St Paul's, Hainault."

Anne and I had felt, after Jim Rattenbury's prophecy, that, to use the words of John Wesley, "the world was our parish." I agreed with the Bishop in his conclusions. I decided to resign the parish at Hainault and live by faith, doing the Lord's work entirely free of pastoral responsibilities. I was called now, not to be a pastor, but to be an evangelist. Anne, after prayer, agreed that this was to be our future. The Bishop promised all the support that he could give, especially as we still hoped to live in the Hainault area and be under his pastoral care, being sustained also by St Paul's.

At first it appeared that this hope would be realised. I would, it seemed, still conduct the Tuesday meetings. It was after I had resigned, however, that the Bishop stated that, in fairness to whoever succeeded me, this arrangement would not work. It was therefore with a mixture of sadness yet hope for the future, that we left St Paul's and moved into Ilford with what was already a full diary of engagements for the year ahead.

Chapter 17

The Holy Spirit operating in the British Isles

Invitations literally poured in from all over England for us to conduct what we called 'Power, Praise and Healing' meetings over long weekends in churches of all denominations. Our first meetings were in Stamford, Lincolnshire, where we now live.

Our visiting there began with a lady who had come to St Paul's, Hainault, from Stamford and who was very ill indeed. She was having to consume over forty tablets a day to keep her alive. Amongst other illnesses she suffered from life-threatening heart disease. As I prayed over her at our church, she fell to the floor, where she lay prone for about twenty minutes. She was so still that her husband, seated in the church, kept looking at her, as I did myself, to see if she was actually alive. Eventually she jumped up and cried out, "I'm healed! I want to throw all my tablets away down the drain!"

We took her back to the vicarage where I counselled her to the effect that I didn't think it was wise to dispense with her tablets until she had had a medical examination. She reluctantly concurred and agreed to seek the advice of her doctor in Stamford. A few days later he declared that all her illnesses had been completely healed and that medication was no longer necessary. She testified to friends about the power and love of God. A lady who worked as a home-help had previously been commissioned by the local health authority to undertake her household chores. However, when she arrived at the home she found her patient fit and well, her services no longer being required.

The story of the miracle appeared in the 'Stamford Mercury', and a local fellowship which was interested in Divine Healing ministry invited us to hold meetings in Stamford. We were happy to accept the offer and subsequently held monthly meetings which so filled the Congregational Hall in Broad Street, that we had to move to the much larger Methodist Church in Barn Hill, where hundreds from Stamford, the Midlands, and all over Lincolnshire packed the building every month for several years, until demands elsewhere meant that we couldn't continue this regular ministry.

The man who took over from us, Alec Jackman, had been healed of a crippling spinal disease, and his son was healed of asthma through our ministry. This man became wonderfully anointed by the Lord as he testified in his men's outfitters shop in Stamford, and indeed in the whole locality. He became very effective in an evangelistic and healing ministry.

Denis Rose was another who began to exercise a healing ministry following a remarkable healing, having suffered from serious kidney disease. He and his wife, Iris, also became dear friends of ours.

Rosalind Allen was a further person who entered into blessing and then into a ministry as a result of the Stamford meetings. This dear lady was walking through Woolworth's at Stamford on a Saturday morning after our Friday gathering when she spotted Anne, who was also in the store. She herself relates what happened in her book, *Out of the Ark*. She writes that she heard a voice saying:

"'Talk to her and ask her about this "something more" (the baptism in the Holy Spirit).'

"'On a Saturday morning, among all the shoppers? No!'

"'I said, talk to her.'

"'Well, only if she is standing there when we have made a full circuit of the sweet course.'

"Of course, she was; and I did.

"Anne has told me since how she had indeed seen me in the gallery the night before. She had wanted to help me then. Now all the advice she could give after these tremendous displays of God's power at work in people's lives was:

'Go home and gather around you a little group of friends who will pray and read the Bible with you.'

"It seemed too trite, too straightforward and, among the friends I had, far too difficult."

Rosalind went on to state that she obeyed this prompting and found it to be 'of the Lord'. Out of their encounter and her experiences at the meeting, grew eventually her nation-wide network of a free Christian book lending service to houses all over the countryside -- the 'Good News Vans'.

"You know, except for you and Anne, all this would never have happened," she later explained.

We praised God for further fruit for our labours. As Jesus said:

"I chose you and appointed you to go and bear fruit -- fruit that will last" (John 15 v 16).

Quite near to Stamford geographically is the town of Wisbech. Here the Methodist Church invited us to take a mission in their 'Elim' Church. It was here, early in our faith ministry, that Anne, my wonderful, superlative wife, began herself to lay hands upon the sick. It happened at the time in the service when I invited sick people to come forward for prayer. A very long queue immediately formed which stretched into the road outside the church. I felt overwhelmed, and when I saw Anne sitting in an attitude of prayer on the front row of the church, I felt led by the Lord to call her out to help me.

Although she had felt nudges from the Lord in this direction, she was surprised, indeed startled, because we had never discussed this possibility and she had never been one to push herself into the limelight. However, she complied with my request. The first person on whom she laid her hands was a very tall and heavy man. The moment she touched him, he went crashing to the floor. This same phenomenon occurred with all those for whom she prayed. Many declared that they had also been healed -- so Anne's healing ministry alongside myself as a husband-and-wife team had begun wonderfully!

Since that time several ministers have declared this 'one-flesh' ministry to be indeed beautiful and effective and have begun their own joint ministry with their wives.

Our work of faith eventually took us all over the British Isles, into every major city and town as well as into many rural areas. It was from one such, Poughill, Cornwall, that the vicar wrote after our visit there:

"It hardly seems possible that already more than three months have gone by since you were with us. So much has happened because of your visit. We have experienced a new freedom in the church and almost every week someone has been born again, healed or set free in some way. Helen was quite ill with some kidney disorder and came to the evening service. You prayed with her, Anne, and she has been well since, and two weeks later she came forward in our Evening Service for salvation. Her husband was born again the following week and they are both going on with the Lord and rejoicing in Him.

"Little Zoe, the baby Trevor prayed with on Sunday morning, was wonderfully healed. Another eighteen month old baby was healed of meningitis and tonsillitis and was out of hospital in three days. His mother was born again last Sunday week. Something good is happening all the time."

Keith Dixon wrote from Whitely Bay, Northumberland:

"I write on behalf of the Whitely Bay Chapter of the Full Gospel Businessmen's Fellowship to thank you most sincerely for the special time you spent with us. It can only be described as tremendous, in many kinds of ways.

"Both evenings were really special, and the fact that you managed to keep them both different and avoided duplication meant that the interest for those able to get to both events was twice as good! Many said how honest and unassuming Trevor sounded, which I am sure enhanced the message.

Anne you were so frank and humble, that you also were quite incredible to listen to.

"It was fabulous to watch you both ministering, we felt very privileged indeed to be able to watch and be allowed to participate in such a special time -- and how many different kinds of people seem to have benefited in so many different ways.

"One small thing which meant so much to my wife and I was that my mother-in-law, bereaved earlier this year, who was formerly very reluctant to have anything to do with Churches and thought we were weird, has been touched by God. She has been explaining how peaceful she has been feeling and has talked extensively about the whole Friday evening she was at, and I know it is for her a new beginning. She suffered from nerves and phobias for much of her life.

"As a born again Christian since 19 years of age (now 39), I cannot remember having had such a spiritual blessing for such a very long time."

From Ashburnham in Sussex a woman wrote after our visit:

"I just want to let you know that Jesus healed me in both areas that Trevor prayed for. When I went to have my blood pressure checked this morning I was allowed to discontinue the wretched pills! And then I went to the eye man and he was left speechless at the improvement. In both cases I was able to witness and say that I knew I had been healed when I was prayed for. Now I feel like shouting it from the roof-tops!"

From Halesowen:

"My wife was especially blessed by your special word for her on Saturday evening. She had already been forward for healing regarding her bladder problem (getting up three or four times In the night). Since your ministry she has had no problems. Praise the Lord."

From Callington, Cornwall:

"I am writing to you out of a heart that is full of thanks and appreciation to God for your ministries amongst us over the last ten days. We are getting reports daily of lives that have been changed through the ministry of the Word of God and through the gifts of the Holy Spirit. People have been saved, taken deeper into the realm of the Holy Spirit, others have spoken of healing for the body and the mind."

From St Mary's Church, Radcliffe-on-Trent, Nottinghamshire:

"We have heard most encouraging testimonies of God's working in peoples' lives both during and following your visit and we believe this marks a significant spiritual milestone in the growth of our fellowship. The timing of your visit could not have been more appropriate and we believe that the result will be a widespread new commitment to Jesus Christ and to His work."

From Hodge Hill, Stourbridge:

"My husband Derek asked you to pray for me because I was suffering from spondylitis in my neck. You said 'spondylitis go' and it did! I could not believe it at first, that it had happened to me. Now I can walk, drive, swim, iron, hoover, and hold my head up without pain. I do not have to lie on the floor for hours to give my neck muscles a rest just to do normal house work."

Not only miracles of healing, but 'exorcisms' continued through our ministry after we left St Paul's, Hainault. Here is one example as reported by Rev George Palmer, a Methodist minister:

28 FEBRUARY 1980 -- LEYLAND ROAD METHODIST CHURCH, SOUTHPORT, MERSEYSIDE

"Two days of meetings and seminars had been arranged and the Rev Trevor Dearing and his wife Anne had been invited to lead the event, the theme being 'Healing and Deliverance'.

"On the first of the two evening meetings I was standing

at the door of the church welcoming the congregation, when a Methodist minister came into the church, drew me aside, and declared, 'We have got problems'. He went on to explain that a coach party of people had come from his church in Skelmersdale, near Wigan, and that one of the passengers was a woman who claimed she was possessed with an evil spirit. Trevor and Anne had just arrived at the church and were preparing for the meeting in the vestry. I asked the minister to wait with his church party until I had consulted with Trevor. This was the first occasion which I had organised such an event and I was confused about the right course of action to take. Trevor said he would see the woman in the vestry, with her husband and minister, but she was not to be brought through the church. I asked one of the church stewards if she would direct the woman to the vestry where I would be to meet them and introduce them to Trevor. What I saw was quite shocking. The woman was being carried by her husband, minister and another friend. She was in a 'ball', her legs and arms drawn tight into her body, hands looking like claws and a look of agony on her face. She was placed into a chair whilst Trevor talked to the people who brought her to him. He enquired from the husband what name she gave to the evil spirit, the husband replied 'Death'. Trevor took hold of the woman, lifted her from the chair and with authority said, 'Spirit of Death, in the name of Jesus Christ I command you to leave this woman and depart to the place prepared for you until the coming of Jesus'. The woman fell to the ground and lay motionless.

"Trevor knelt beside her and prayed for the Holy Spirit to come upon her. After a few moments she opened her eyes and gave a beautiful smile. She was lifted to her feet and everyone embraced her. She declared, 'I am free! I am free!'. Trevor invited the woman to return to the congregation but to allow God to minister gently to her during the service.

The service was timed to begin at 7.30. I took the woman into the vestry at 7.20. The meeting began at exactly the appointed time. This wonderful event took place in approximately 7 minutes.

"I was reduced to tears as I saw for the very first time the accounts recorded in the Gospels of Jesus releasing those who were demon possessed before my eyes. The church steward had returned to the church door and the woman and those with her went back the way they had come to the vestry. So amazed was the church steward by what she saw she went and brought others who had also seen the woman arrive at the church to show to them the remarkable change which had taken place in the woman's life.

"Whenever I saw the Methodist minister [of that church] after that remarkable experience he would tell me of the progress being made by the woman and her husband. They became involved in the church, becoming members. The news of the woman was always encouraging. After about 3 years the minister moved to another circuit and I lost contact with the situation. I shall never forget that remarkable moment when I saw the power of God at work through one of his servants -- this is the Lord's doing and it is marvellous in our eyes."

A unique healing, which took place in the Floral Hall in Coventry, is also worth recording. The meeting was coming to a close with the singing of loud, rhythmic praises to God, when, to my astonishment, nearly everyone left their seats and began to dance as they sang. As I watched from the platform it seemed that I was beholding a sort of spiritual discotheque.

"How does one bring a meeting like this to a close?" I thought. "I certainly wasn't taught how to do it at my Theological College!"

Just then my own feet spontaneously began to move in

time to the music. Before long my legs were following suit. The thought came into my mind, "David danced before the Lord with all his might -- why shouldn't a parson do the same?"

I ran down the platform steps and grabbed hold of the nearest lady, who happened to be both middle-aged and plump. I began swinging her around as we continued singing our praises. Then some recognition of her came to me.

"Haven't-I-seen-you-somewhere-before?" I enquired in time to the music.

"Yes-you've-seen-me-somewhere-before-and-isn't-Jesus-wonderful," she chanted.

"Where-have-I-seen-you-somewhere-before?" I sang. "Glory to God in the highest!"

"You've-seen-me-in-the-wheelchair-over-there!" she sang.

I stopped dancing.

"What has happened?" I excitedly questioned.

"Well," she said, this time very calmly, "I've been paralysed for fourteen years, and when you laid hands on me in the meeting, nothing happened. But when people started to dance I felt my legs begin to move, and the next thing I knew, I was dancing with you."

"Surely God inhabits the praises of His people," I replied, full of awe and wonder.

These are merely samples of accounts of God moving through our ministry all over the land. We were ministering in the truth of the Kingdom of God, not just in a special church situation. We know it because of the lasting fruit of the message and ministry.

Chapter 18
Miracles overseas

Anne and I have taken three missions altogether in the dioceses of Singapore and Malaysia. The first two were at the invitation of Bishop Chu Ban It and the third was when we were asked by his successor Bishop Moses Tai to minister as evangelists at the Anglican Conference on World Evangelisation in 1992. All, we are told, have had a profound influence on the spiritual life and mission, especially in the diocese of Singapore.

On our first visit there we were very surprised by the intensity of the climate. Although we had been warned that it would be hot, we had not been prepared for the humidity.

"It's like a perpetual Turkish bath," I remarked to Anne.

"Yes," she replied, somewhat concerned, "how will we be able to minister in this climate without being exhausted?"

We discovered, as we missioned, that all the churches, and the Cathedral, had their windows wide open and fans revolving at their fastest speed during our meetings. But still our light clothes stuck to our flesh.

After our first visit we returned on a follow-up crusade in March 1978, and this time the mission was concentrated on the grounds outside the Cathedral. Many hundreds of people gathered together for the meetings, and scores sought Christ as their Saviour, with a large number receiving ministry for healing, including seekers from other religions.

One dramatic account of the meetings and miracles of healing comes from Mrs Chen Ti Wen. Her story appeared in the Christian magazine, 'Asian Beacon':

"'I was an insomniac. For over three years I had broken nights and fitful sleep. As the night hours ticked away, I feared I would not have enough sleep and would have trouble waking up the next morning. On the other hand, I dared not go to bed early for fear that I might be awakened by some noise and then I would have to stay awake till dawn. As a result, my health was very poor. I was always down with the 'flu. I developed bronchitis and came down with pneumonia. All the time I was consulting doctors, my insomnia was getting worse. I became very depressed.

I Joined the Queue

"'Then one day I received a pamphlet announcing some power, praise and healing meeting being conducted by a certain Rev Trevor Dearing, an Anglican priest from England. There would be a message and prayers for the sick. I was interested to attend, so both my husband and I went to St James Church for the meeting. The church was packed with people but because we were early, we managed to get seats quite close to the front.

"'"It is finished" -- that was the topic of the message that night. Jesus said these words when He was on the cross of Calvary. Rev Dearing preached, "Jesus Christ has finished the work of redemption on the cross of Calvary. He has finished taking away our burdens, our fears, our troubles, griefs and sorrows. The only thing you need to do is to come to Jesus and receive from Him what He has already done for you on the cross nearly 2000 years ago."

"'He preached the message with power. After that, he invited people with needs to go forward for prayers. Soon, there was a very long queue. I sat in my seat watching him pray for the sick.

"'When the queue was getting shorter I told my husband, "I wish the preacher to pray for me also."

"'My husband accompanied me to join the queue. As I stood in line I prayed and prepared my heart before the Lord. When my turn came, Rev Dearing laid his hand on my head and prayed for me. My two legs became soft and I could no longer stand. Someone behind me helped me to lie down on the floor. When I opened my eyes, I saw my husband standing beside me. I raised my hand and he tried to lift me. However, I just had no strength to get up.

It can't be Nine o'Clock!

"'Then I heard someone say to my husband, "Let her rest for a while." I continued to pray on the floor. After some time, I got up by myself. I was filled with peace and I knew it was the perfect peace the Lord Jesus had promised His disciples, "Peace I leave with you, my peace I give unto you, not as the world giveth, give I unto you." (Jn 14:27)

"'It was nearly twelve midnight when we reached home that night. I quickly prepared myself for bed. Previously, when it was around this time I would fear that I might be late getting up the next day. Yet, I dared not go to bed early for fear that I might be awakened by some noise and then I would have to stay awake until dawn. That night, I fell asleep easily. When I woke up the next morning, I looked at my watch. It was nine o'clock! I told myself the watch must be wrong. So I went to the sitting room to look at the wall clock. The clock showed nine o'clock. The truth hit me: I had slept for nine uninterrupted hours! For more than three years now, I had never slept for so many hours in a single night. From that night, the 4th March 1978 onwards, I have been able to sleep restfully every night. In time, my other sicknesses disappeared. I thank and praise the Lord that I am now well and healthy.

A Very Slow Learner

"'The Lord's mighty hand of healing did not touch me alone. He also touched and healed my third son, Jer Hueih, who was mentally retarded. Jer Hueih was born a normal and healthy baby. When he was about a year old, he developed very high fever. The doctor who saw him for two days advised that he should be sent to hospital. My husband

and I brought him to Alexandra Hospital where he was hospitalised for 10 days. I stayed in the hospital with him. His fever continued to be high for many days and on several occasions, the nurses had to sponge him with iced water.

"'After 10 days, he was discharged from the hospital. At home, my husband and I found that our son could not talk. Before he was ill, he could call Papa, Mama and Chacha (the maid who helped to look after him). But now, he could not call any of us. About a year or so later, he learned to talk again, but we observed that he was a very slow learner. When he was four and a half years old, he could not recognise a single number or a single letter of the alphabet. This was despite the fact that being a school teacher myself, I tried hard to teach him. He also had a dull look on his face. Often, he would sit by himself with his mouth half-open and his tongue slightly jutting out. I was grieved and my worries and grief over my son's condition had partly contributed to my earlier insomnia.

"'A few days after I was healed of my insomnia, my husband and I brought our three sons, our maid and a friend to another power, praise and healing meeting. This time the meeting was held at the St Andrew's Cathedral. Rev Trevor Dearing preached and after he had finished, he invited the people to go forward for prayers. This time I did not hesitate. I got up, and carrying my third son, who was then four and a half years old, I joined the queue. My two older sons, aged seven and eight, were in front of me. My husband, although he was not sick, had also walked up and he was in front of us.

"'As we stood in line, I told my three children, "The pastor is going to pray for us soon. You need not be afraid. The Lord is going to bless us." They nodded their heads in agreement.

He Can Add!

"'When our turn came, I let Jer Hueih stand together with his brothers. Rev Dearing touched their heads. All the three boys fell to the floor as the power of the Holy Spirit came upon them. After some time, they got up by themselves. On our way home, the boys happily sang choruses in the car. Then they talked amongst themselves, "It is very strange. Just now we were lying on the floor, but, it was just like lying on our own bed." I suppose they had felt the same peace and comfort as I had felt when God's power was upon me.

"'For the next few days, I noticed that my third son, Jer Hueih, slept a great deal. He would wake up for his meals, play a little while and then go to sleep again.

"'About two and a half months later, my eldest son Jew Yaw, who was in Primary Three, came to me and said, "Mummy, Hueih can do additions!"

"'I knew Hueih could not add because he could not even recognise the numbers. So, I just smiled and said, "Oh, who taught him?"

"'My eldest son said, "I taught him." Then he brought me a pencil and a piece of paper and said, "Mummy, you write out simple sums on the paper and ask Hueih for the answers."

"'I wrote: $1 + 2 =$. Hueih said "Three."

"'At first, I thought Hueih had shouted the right answer by chance. So I wrote down another simple sum. Again, he was correct. He could also recognise the numbers from 1 to 5. I was truly amazed. In the days that followed, I taught him more numbers and also the alphabet. To my great surprise, he could remember what I taught him and could learn very fast.

God's Amazing Grace

"'Jer Hueih is now twelve years old. He is in Secondary One. Ever since he went to school, from Primary One to

Primary Six, the marks in his report books always averaged 90% and above. Last year, he sat for the Primary School Leaving Examination (PSLE). He was among the top ten percent of pupils who passed the PSLE. Praise the Lord!

"'I know it was the Lord our God who touched him and made him whole. Whenever I look at my son and recall how the Lord has healed him and how He has healed me, my heart and spirit would just adore and worship Him.

"'Truly, the Lord Jesus Christ is the same yesterday, today and forever (Heb 13:8).'

"Mrs Chen is a school teacher in Singapore. Her husband, Dr Chen is an associate professor, Zoology Department, at the National University of Singapore. They have four sons. The youngest, Jer Ming, was born 1½ years after Mrs Chen was healed of her insomnia."

The mission in 1992 was once again mainly in the grounds of the Singapore Cathedral and, once again, many hundreds gathered to hear me preach the 'full Gospel' of the New Birth, Healing, Baptism in the Holy Spirit and Deliverance. Many lives were affected, as is illustrated from a letter of testimony from Mr and Mrs Ivor and Rosemary Williams:

"My wife (Rosemary) and I were in Singapore in September on our way to visiting our extended families in Australia.

"On Sunday 2 September I asked my hotel porter for the way to the nearest RC church. He directed me across the road to St Andrew's Cathedral. I felt sure that he was mistaken but nevertheless went there, to find that a World Evangelical Congress was about to start.

"That night, after mass at the RC cathedral, we went to the first of your three evening meetings. We also went to the second and third, and have the tapes of all three. We now see ourselves as 'Born Again Catholics' and have had the opportunity, in our local church, to make our witness for Christ as co-leaders of a local group at the final (seven-part) session of a diocesan Renew programme. As the topic was Evangelisation, we had every chance to remind people of the Good News which some of them had forgotten.

"After the Singapore congress we were fortunate enough to meet and spend some time with the Rev Alan Maddox (from Western Australia) who was on an exchange visit to Singapore. He helped us a great deal. But we had wanted to get in touch with you. I have just got your address through the Evangelical Alliance.

"We specially want to thank you and your wife Anne for the wonderful events of Singapore, which have changed our lives dramatically.

"In Brisbane it was a great joy to us to be at one with our daughter's family, who are RC Charismatics and 'in the Kingdom', as you put it. So their prayers on our behalf had been answered, as had those of our youngest son, who is a member of Cobham Christian Fellowship.

"I recently met a very very senior Jesuit who was visiting in our area. I managed to speak to him privately and told him of our Singapore experience. I know it will not greatly surprise you that he was delighted. Wonderful things are happening.

"(PS: My wife stood up on Night 1. It took me another two days, but I made it on Night 3! I shall be 70 on Christmas Day -- it will be very special.)"

On the last two occasions of visiting Singapore, we followed up the mission there with visits to the diocese of Malaysia. In 1992 we actually missioned in the Cathedral in Kuala Lumpur, and once again I found myself teaching the Bishop and clergy the truths of the Full Gospel.

Our visits to Singapore were also occasions of dramatic

deliverance (exorcism) ministry. On our first mission we were called upon to drive the evil spirits out of a young girl who kept going into trances. She explained also that every night when she went to sleep she was visited by a rider on a black horse who announced to her that she was going to die. She always awoke at exactly the same time, 2.00 a.m., shaking with terror. After ministry the trances and the visitations ceased.

On our second visit, I had to drive a spirit out of an Indian man who came to a meeting in the Hilton Hotel. He became violent during the ministry and tried to attack me. I claimed the protection of the Lord and, try as he would, he couldn't hurt me. He became a dedicated Christian after effective deliverance ministry.

More exorcism took place in the Singapore prison. We were invited to hold a meeting there for the inmates, and the recreation hall was crammed full with male prisoners. I preached to them about the freedom that there is in Christ when we repent and believe the Gospel. Many came forward to accept Christ as their Saviour. As I began to minister to them however, several fell on the floor and began hissing, banging their heads on the concrete and squirming like snakes. I ministered deliverance to each one in the Name of Jesus and they became calm and peaceful as they were set free. I later learned that they had belonged to a Satanic cult, worshipping the devil in the form of a snake, but now they turned to Christ.

The 'come-back' we have had is that our missions to the Far East were graciously used by God to the furtherance of His Kingdom and that the movement of the Spirit, which began with our visits there, has intensified and spread all over that part of the world.

In 1976 I was invited to be a speaker and to minister to peoples' needs at the World Conference of the Holy Spirit in Jerusalem sponsored by Logos International of the USA. This was followed by further invitations to similar Conferences in the

following two years.   On the second of these we saw a
remarkable move of the Spirit of God as, after I had preached,
He began to move amongst the congregation in spontaneous acts
of healing.   One after the other, believers stood to their feet
declaring that they had been healed.   All this provoked a great
deal of excitement amidst rapturous praise to God by the
congregation.

Eventually the meeting seemed to come to an end and I
said what was meant to be a final prayer.   Just then however,
Anne stood up and uttered a prophecy.   In this she said that
God was calling Jewish people present, and who had been
undecided about whether Jesus was the Messiah, to come forward and yield their lives to Him.   About twenty people
answered this call to commitment, running forward and kneeling
at the front of the hall of meeting.   Some were weeping openly
as these Jewish seekers completed their faith by accepting Jesus
as their Saviour and Lord.

I preached at these gatherings to people from all over the
world, being translated into ten different languages.   Often we
were ministering healing until the early hours of the morning.

The concluding World Conference of the Holy Spirit was
in Switzerland where, once again, we were given the leadership
in preaching and the healing ministry.   We had to have special
Services of Healing to deal with all the people.   Our ministry at
this Conference led to further invitations to minister all over
Switzerland in Anglican and other churches, where we saw God
move in power.

It was at the Swiss Conference that Anne had an unusual
experience.   Because she couldn't speak any languages except
English she ministered to seekers by praying in tongues over
them.   One lady, who proved to be from South America, later
told Anne, through an interpreter, that she had heard her pray
over her in fluent Spanish and that in this language she had, in
the Spirit, described her need to be freed from the influence of

witchcraft and be healed of a chronic stomach condition. Both these prayers had, in fact, been instantly answered and the woman, previously an agnostic, gave her life to Jesus.

The World Conference in Jerusalem also led to our being invited to mission in Finland. This was by invitation of Patmos International. We paid two month-long visits to this country, travelling the length and breadth of the land. Lutheran Churches and secular halls were packed by seekers, who often stood outside if they could not get into the building. We were amazed at the way in which the Holy Spirit moved through our ministry as people pressed in upon us, and scores fell to the ground and were healed as we laid our hands upon them.

One remarkable miracle which happened through Anne's ministry was when a woman who had been born blind, began to shout, in her Finnish language, that she could see light. Her testimony appeared in a continental Christian magazine.

The Conferences in Jerusalem also opened doors for us to mission in the United States of America. On our way to our first ministry in that great country however, we stopped off the plane to take meetings on the island of Bermuda. These meetings were initiated by the Full Gospel Businessmen's Fellowship. Here also, meeting halls were packed to capacity, and details of our visit and photographs of ourselves appeared on the front page of the national daily newspaper.

As we were leaving the island for the USA we had to pass through American customs. One of the customs officers opened my case and then gave me a long hard look.

"Aren't you the healing man from England?" he asked.

"You could call me that, but I minister the healing that comes from Jesus," I replied.

"Can you do anything for my back?" he further enquired. "I'm in agonies of pain bending over these cases."

"Bend your head and take off your cap," I exhorted.

He followed my instructions and I laid my hands on his

head, commanding that his back be healed in the Name of Jesus. After a few moments, he straightened up and delightedly exclaimed, "It's gone, all the pain has gone! Will it last until I go off duty?"

"Jesus's healing is for life," I explained. "Trust in the Lord and you will be well."

With that we departed for our flight.

Our visit to Bermuda is marked by a healing also of a cat! Anne had visited a house meeting in order to give her testimony to a group of ladies. The host had introduced Anne to her lovely large Persian cat, which, she sadly told Anne, was incurably sick.

"She always used to attend our Christian meetings in the home," said the lady. "Do you believe God could heal an animal?"

"All things are possible to Him," declared Anne as she laid hands on the stricken cat and prayed that God would heal one of His lovely creatures.

On our return to England we received a letter and photo of the cat, stating that it had been completely healed and was attending the meetings once again. This was the first instance of many of the healing of animals through our ministry. Another I remember well was a large dog named 'Benji' which couldn't use its hind legs. After prayer it stood on them alone as it reached up to lick my face.

In all we undertook three ministry tours of the United States. The first consisted mainly of speaking at 'Full Gospel' Christian dinners and the North Carolina Christian Convention. We also appeared on television, when I gave my testimony on the "P[raise] T[he] L[ord] Club" programme.

The next two tours were mainly of Episcopal Churches, for Christian Renewal and Healing meetings. All were wonderfully blessed by the Lord. Worthy of mention is Anne's ministry to an unbelieving husband and his Christian wife, who were on the verge of divorce. Their marriage, like many couples' marriages about which we have prayed, was marvellously restored to mutual love. In this case the husband became a Christian.

Our ministry overseas during the years has not only included churches, dinners in hotels, television and radio ministry, but also schools, universities, meetings of doctors and also of clergy. In all we have seen the God of Truth wonderfully at work, revealing Himself as a living God whose interest and grace reaches every area of the globe and every human life in all its aspects and concerns.

One man and his wife who were deeply touched by God in America were undergoing marital difficulties. The wife told the story to a Christian magazine, describing firstly, a fresh attempt to live in reconciliation with her husband, in the words:

"I found myself in a dilemma. I wanted Shaine to grow up in a home with both her father and mother. And I still loved Paul, who was obviously suffering. Finally, I agreed. But when Paul returned home our struggles were far from over. A restlessness still gnawed at him; he was jittery, distracted, still drinking. Whenever I suggested that we pray or read the Bible or go to prayer meeting, he shook his head.

"'Paul,' I begged, 'we both need a new knowledge deeper than human understanding. Someone stronger than human strength. We need Jesus Christ.'

"He looked at me intently. 'You've found your way down that road, Debbie,' he said, 'but it's not for me.' He paused. 'Yes, I believe in Christ,' he added. 'But at this point He isn't very much part of my life, is He?' I could almost feel the pain in his eyes.

"'Please, Paul,' I said, 'please come to church with me.' His face flamed. He rose and stalked away, shouting over his shoulder, 'Why do you keep trying to drag me to prayer meetings all the time?'

"In despair, I turned to Paul's mother for solace. One afternoon after she let me sob my heart out, she said, 'Are you sure you're placing Paul in God's hands? Remember when you prayed for another child? God heard you.'

"Then she leaned forward. 'One thing I do know; Paul is like many men, even when he was a little boy he was stubborn. The more we tried to push him, the more stubborn he became.' She touched my arm. 'Why don't you give him up to God?'

"I knew deep down she was right. No one can follow another person's path to Christ. Each of us has to find his own way.

"And from then on I relinquished him to God. For a whole year I began all my prayers with, 'Lord, enter Paul's heart as You came into mine. I will help in any way You choose.' Life was more peaceful after that, but Paul was still suffering.

"Then a visiting clergyman from England, the Reverend Trevor Dearing, came to our church. I thought Paul might be interested in hearing a speaker from another part of the world. But when I told Paul about Father Dearing I could see the old fire rise in his eyes and I quickly backed off.

"However, on the following Sunday, as I was leaving for church, Paul stopped me at the door. 'I'll go with you,' he said, adding quickly, 'but just this once.'

"I was elated, but hid my feelings. Once in church I could sense his resistance to everything taking place. He sat there stiff, scowling, silent when the hymns were sung. He heard the call to the altar, watched people answer it. Then, to my amazement, Paul rose slowly and moved down the aisle. 'Oh Lord, he needs Your help,' I prayed. But when the clergyman placed his hands on Paul's head, he just stiffly stood there, turned and hurried back to my side.

"On the way home he was silent for a time, then quietly

said, 'I walked down the aisle because I wanted to cleanse myself of all the wrong I did and the hurt I gave you. But when Father Dearing put his hands on my head I was sceptical that anything could happen. Deb, I just couldn't open my heart.'

"I prayed for the right words to say. 'Will . . . will you come with me again?' I ventured.

"'Maybe. I don't know.' And then he added almost under his breath, 'I've watched you over the past year, Deb, and you've become so sure, so serene. I wish I could feel the way you do.'

"The following Sunday night Paul decided on his own to attend the prayer meeting. In church Father Dearing and his wife, Ann, were at the altar. When Father Dearing began talking, Paul listened intently. He hunched forward when Father Dearing talked of, 'our inner prison, a prison of our own making. We all want to escape it, but even the most powerful cannot escape it alone. There is only One who can give us the key.' Then he invited everyone who had not yet met Jesus to come and meet Him.

"Paul stood up. His face was pale, his eyes shining; his fingers gripped my arm. 'Deb, come with me,' he said softly. I rose and he placed me in front of him, still holding my arm. We followed the first few people down the aisle. At the altar he stood behind me. I heard a noise. I turned. Paul lay on the floor. People were praying over him. Then he got up slowly and led me back to our seats. He was all right but I was mystified as to what had happened to him.

"When the meeting was over Paul hurried both of us outside. 'I wasn't sure anything would happen,' he said, his face flushed, his speech rapid, as though he wanted to tell it all at once.

"'But when Mrs Dearing put her hands on my head, I felt a surge of peace sweep through me like a big ocean wave. All of my strength left me. Next thing I knew I was on my back, looking up at a ring of faces praying. My mind cleared and I knew I had surrendered myself to the presence of God.'

"Paul's face was filled with a new light. He looked serene, at peace. He crushed me to him and said huskily, 'Deb, I felt as if I were resting in the hands of the Lord!'

"'You were, Paul,' I said joyously. 'You are!'

"Since that day, God's hand has been on Paul. His inner turmoil is gone. Of course, our problems didn't all disappear, nor did our marriage become all sweetness and light. But now the two of us are working on them together.

"My most important lesson was learning that not I nor anyone else could determine his salvation or mine. Only God could do that. I could only pray that He would reach a loved one who had wandered away from Him.

"Together, Paul and I have found a knowledge deeper than human understanding, and Someone stronger than any human strength."

PART FOUR

Burnt out for Jesus

Chapter 19
The call to America

It was while we were on our last tour of America that I began to experience very severe chest pains. I sat at the airport in Orlando, awaiting our flight to Ocala, Florida, feeling very ill. When we arrived at our destination I went immediately to the emergency department of the local hospital and was admitted with a suspected heart attack.

Anne was, naturally, extremely anxious, but bravely took the whole of our scheduled meeting in a packed church that evening, where she gave her testimony and ministered to many people, including a Methodist minister who received the baptism of the Holy Spirit through her prayers.

The next morning, after a great many tests, I was discharged from the hospital and continued with our mission, still feeling far from well. This was to prove to be the gradual onset of a serious and disabling sickness.

Whilst we were in Ocala, the rector there, who was our host, informed us that the internationally known rector of St Luke's Episcopal Church, Seattle, the Reverend Dennis Bennett, was due to retire, and that the church there was searching for a priest to be his successor. He asked if we were interested. Was I interested! At first the thought took my breath away -- but would it be what the Lord wanted? The proposition led us to pray for His guidance as to whether we should put our names before St Luke's Search Committee, but we were, at this stage, far from sure that it would be the right action for our future.

On our return home I experienced chest pains again and went to consult my doctor about my health. He told me that he considered my pains to be caused by massive overwork and that my stress tolerance was very low.

"Haven't you considered giving up itinerant work and settling down to ministry as a pastor in a church?" he enquired.

Anne and I prayed about this and felt that through the rector in Ocala and our Christian doctor, God was truly speaking to us about a change of ministry; but was it to be in America?

The first person I had to consult was my own Bishop, who was, now that we lived in his diocese, the Bishop of Peterborough. I put the whole situation to him and he said that he thought we ought to apply to St Luke's, Seattle.

His advice in fact, placed us in the most critical dilemma that we had ever faced in our lives, as we thought about the situation of our family. Rebecca had married Nicholas, a prospective chartered accountant, and lived in Ilford, Essex, where she was expecting her first child. Rachael had already planned her wedding to John, a fine, handsome and dependable young man in Margate, Kent, where she lived and worked in a bank. Ruth was a staff nurse at the London Hospital, and Philip, who was still at home with us, was studying for his 'O' levels at Stamford Boys' Grammar School. None of them was in a position to come with us to America if we decided to go, and our emigration would mean leaving the whole family behind. Our children did not at all like the prospect of this happening; and neither did we, as we had always been very close in our relationships.

In view of my health and the family situation we decided to take two steps. The first was to actually apply to St Luke's to see what they felt to be the will of God in calling us to be their rector amongst the other hundred priests who were seeking the position. If St Luke's gave us a negative response then we would know God had shut that door. The other action was to approach the Reverend John Trillo, Bishop of Chelmsford, who had always been very supportive of our ministry at Hainault and as itinerants, to see if he felt he had a place in his diocese. We also sought the advice of the Bishop of Lincoln in whose diocese was St Mary's Church, Stamford, where we worshipped when at home. We, of course, committed all this to the Lord and felt we would know his will. Obedience to God had never been our problem, but we wished God would write on the wall what he wanted us to do!

As events unfolded, the Bishop of Chelmsford and the Bishop of Lincoln both felt that my ministry was so different from the Church of England norm that they couldn't find a place where we would fit in. On the other hand the Search Committee at St Luke's were keenly interested in us and invited us to go to the United States for a week to meet with them and to see their church in action.

The week at St Luke's showed us that they were an evangelical, charismatic and yet catholic church, where our ministry would fit in like a hand into a glove. It was just the sort of church that I had always hoped for. We had a wonderful week of meetings and interviews, dinners and committees, and came away much impressed with the people, the leaders, their worship and emphasis on the Person and work of the Holy Spirit. Every week there was a meeting where believers testified and ministered the baptism in the Holy Spirit. Healing ministry was also regularly on offer and they were used to seeing the deliverance ministry in operation. The heart of the worship of the church was the Eucharist, when the priest wore vestments and the Sacrament was reserved on the altar. They greatly emphasised a counselling ministry for the healing of memories. Their priest was even called "Father". The only discordant note on the visit was a message from a Churchwarden's wife, which she claimed to be prophetic, that it was not the will of God for us to take up ministry at her church.

Weeks passed by and St Luke's people fasted and prayed to know the will of God as to who was to be their next rector. We were still in agony of mind about what our going to America would mean to our family. We had decided at one point to write to St Luke's withdrawing our application, when that very day we had a telephone call from the Senior Churchwarden, informing us that St Luke's had come to a unanimous conclusion that I was to be their Rector.

We also received two telegrams, one from Reverend Dennis Bennett and one from Father Dick O'Driscoll, who was St Luke's assistant priest, congratulating us on our appointment. The Bishop of Olympia, in whose diocese St Luke's was situated, was also welcoming us into his cure of souls. God, we felt, had made His will known; the Church of England had said 'no'; the Episcopal Church of America had said 'yes'. We would therefore tear ourselves from our family and go to America.

Chapter 20
St Luke's -- Seattle

It was on 10th June 1981 that we boarded the plane at Heathrow bound for our new ministry in Seattle. As we travelled, we reflected on the situation of our family, for leaving our children, Anne said, was like tearing the flesh from her bones. We had placed Philip in lodgings with a friend in Stamford and the plan was that he would take his 'O' levels and then join us for life in America. Ruth was in the nurses' home in London and said that she had no desire to live in America. We had sent out the invitations to Rachael's wedding, planned for October, and she too would stay in England and start a family. Rebecca was heavily pregnant and she, as well as her husband Nicholas, also felt that their future was in England.

However, as we had committed the American venture to God, our house had sold overnight, passports and immigration had gone through without a hitch, and St Luke's had stated that they would pay our air fare twice a year for us to return to England and visit our family, including Anne's mother who was in her seventies. As far as we could understand, we felt that we were in God's will, and perhaps would stay at St Luke's for five to seven years before returning to take up a ministry in England, when we hoped I would fully have regained my health.

When we arrived at Seattle airport there was a party from St Luke's to welcome us to the church. They were cheering and displaying balloons and banners. One read:

GET OUT THE TEAPOT THE BRITISH ARE HERE

We were eventually taken to the rectory which was fully equipped with borrowed furniture and implements for cooking and eating, on loan whilst ours was crossing the Atlantic. However, when everyone had gone, and just the two of us remained, we immediately felt alone and even lost.

I plunged myself into ministry at St Luke's, which I found to be a church of wonderful Spirit-filled believers, which urgently needed building up as a real Christian community, as an expression of the Body of Christ. To this end I started a fellowship meeting on a Wednesday evening where believers could share together the joys and trials of their Christian pilgrimage. I also started what I called 'Growth Groups' in homes all over the city so that members could meet together in small groups and really get to know their fellow church members at real depth and where they could minister to each other.

The Sunday Services needed little alteration, as our two buildings were packed with worshippers in two glorious 'charismatic' Eucharists. In due course I also began a 'Power, Praise and Healing' meeting on the lines of St Paul's Hainault Tuesday meetings, and once again we overflowed our church with seekers after God's blessing. Thus over two years the church life grew in depth and in numbers, and we also punctuated our programme with social gatherings, which were very happy occasions.

In the first year we received seventy-eight new church members. Our income also grew in a very healthy way and we were able, as a church, to tithe to missions and Christian work outside our own church life. We even sent out missionaries from our church, one of whom was Paula Shields, who is still ministering in Europe.

Anne was in charge of the healing ministry at St Luke's, and every Sunday she and her helpers were powerfully anointed by the Holy Spirit to bring healing to the sick. The church's ministry of inner healing was re-organised and was always working at full stretch to bring peace to those who were troubled in mind and spirit. Anne and I also counselled church members at real depth, and many were released into new joy and freedom.

Our church finances also enabled us to give help, including food, to those who were in financial distress. The abundance of giving by church members enabled me to be assisted by four full-time staff: Dick O'Driscoll the Curate, Marion MacDonald the Church Administrator, Rochelle Bennett the Church Secretary and Bob Peal the Verger. Many more members gave loyal and time-consuming service to the church. In all it proved to be a wonderful work for God.

Soon after our arrival, however, we began to go through some real traumas. The value of the pound dropped dramatically against the dollar, and this meant that we were no longer able to buy a house. The rectory, was, at best, meant only to be a temporary home for us, as the church wanted to sell it. After a great deal of deliberation, wherein we felt that we might have to return to England because we had nowhere to live, the vestry decided they would increase my stipend, completely renovate the rectory and would then sell it to us at a knock-down price. This was a wonderfully loving offer and showed how much they already felt I was the right person in God to be Pastor of the Church. They also already loved Anne and very much appreciated her service for the Lord. Anne felt the same love for them, too!

The house problem was followed by troubles with our plans for the family. Philip came out to join us for his summer vacation and desperately implored us to be allowed to stay with us in America. After much prayer and discussion, we decided that, although he had no academic qualifications as yet, we would place him in Ballard High School and allow him to remain. He soon became very happy in the United States.

This change of plans was followed by long and urgent telephone calls from Rachael in Margate, who was in terrible distress, anxiety and panic and who was obviously going through an emotional breakdown. She was advised by her doctor to come to us in America to see if she could recover. On her arrival it was obvious that the cause of her trouble was that she no longer wanted to marry John, admirable young man though he was.

After much heart-searching and not a little distress, she broke off her engagement, and decided to stay with us permanently in America. After a year Ruth also decided to join us in Seattle, as she was going through a period of emotional upheaval. We finished up, in 1982, with three of our children with us whilst still feeling that we wanted eventually to return to England, but now destined, for our family's sake, to stay in America. Rebecca was also left isolated from us all, with her own family in London.

All this family concern did not help what proved to be my rapidly failing health. It was whilst I was officiating at a mid-week Communion Service that I had my first panic attack. It hit me suddenly, like a bolt from the blue, and was as bad as any I had had in my teenage life. These attacks continued on waking every morning as I shook with terror and fear of I know not what. Soon my whole nervous system seemed to be affected and I began to experience periods of very deep depression with times of shedding tears and crying aloud, for I felt to be in such misery.

Then, after a little while, I began to have excruciating chest pains, and I feared that there was something very wrong with my heart. These attacks of pain took me to a heart specialist and, several times, I was rushed into hospital as an emergency case. All this was extremely worrying for Anne, who supported and nursed me with incredible care and devotion. I became rapidly more sick emotionally and physically until, when on a mission to Dallas, Texas, I completely collapsed -- a physical and mental wreck.

The flight back to Seattle was a nightmare and seemed endless, and on arrival I was immediately hospitalised. I was diagnosed as having a serious chemical condition in my nervous system and also coronary artery spasms which threatened my life. I was given medication which, I was told, could help but not cure me, and I was discharged from hospital still very ill.

I was told that I needed a complete and indefinite rest. Anne and I decided to take a vacation in England for three months, and our friends Denis and Iris Rose were able to find us a lodge to rent. This was in March 1983. We arrived in England and were met at the airport by Pastor Mike Sherwood of the Ilford Elim Church, and by Rebecca. They took us to Rebecca's home where I collapsed in emotional turmoil. I didn't know where I really belonged: in America or in England. Pastor Sherwood prayed, especially with Anne, expressing the agony it must be for her to be nursing a husband in this condition.

I eventually put myself under a British heart specialist and even a psychiatrist to see if they could help. Sadly, my health still deteriorated as it became obvious that I could not return to take up my duties at St Luke's, because I was suffering from a chronic illness. I became increasingly anxious and depressed and was crippled with chest pains. The Churchwardens at St Luke's told me to take a year off, but medical advice was that there was no guarantee I would ever be healthy again. With considerable sadness I resigned my position at the church where we had been privileged to minister in consolidation of the work of Dennis Bennett.

Chapter 21
England again

My illness put a real responsibility upon Anne, who was caring for me in her own devoted way. She, too, became run-down emotionally and physically with the strain of it all. Only those who have nursed a loved one suffering from severe emotional illness can really understand the intense burden it represents. Yet Anne had also other, very practical concerns to which to attend. Firstly, she had to return to Seattle by herself, pack up our home, sell our car, and say our farewells to the church. When, in fact, she arrived in Seattle she was so exhausted that she had to have a complete rest for a week before she could attend to these matters, which also included Philip's graduation from High School.

Ruth and Rachael decided that they would not follow us once again across the Atlantic, but would stay in America to see how life turned out for them. Anne had to establish them with furniture, in an apartment. Philip desperately wanted to stay in the United States, but was still under age. He even thought of joining the American military in order to stay, but eventually agreed to return to England, determined, however, to go back to America at the first opportunity. He eventually did this after he had obtained a Bachelor of Science Degree in Quantity Surveying at Reading University. He now lives permanently in Seattle.

When Anne returned from her packing-up operation, we found that we had enough money in the bank from the sale of our previous home and from what we had saved, to buy a lovely village home in Easton-on-the-Hill near Stamford. We lived there for eleven years before moving into our present home near Stamford town centre.

Anne continued to nurse me, but still had two duties to

attend to in America. Rachael very soon decided to marry Jim, an American man whom she had met and, as I was still too ill to travel, Anne had to fly out to St Luke's to attend this wedding alone. It was as she sat in the church feeling all alone that she felt a hand on her shoulder and heard the voice of the Lord speaking to her, saying:

"I will be a friend and a husband to you now and whenever you need Me."

This gave her a great deal of comfort. Later, when we attended a Conference at Swanwick, Derbyshire, the Right Reverend Richard Hare, Bishop of Pontefract, put his arm around Anne and expressed his sympathy with her in the load she was carrying; it was as though he was confirming the Lord's comforting words.

Soon Anne had to fly out again alone to Seattle for Ruth's wedding to Richard, which once more she found to be a real strain as she realised in a new way that we were again going to be a separated family with, eventually, three of our children living permanently in America. In fact Rachael and Ruth now have two boys each, giving us six grandsons altogether, and they are very happily married, with a very good quality of life out there.

We all, including Rebecca in Ilford, still miss each other very much. Our American families long for us to go and join them to live in the States, but Rebecca, naturally, wants us to stay with her and her family in England; we are, in fact, very settled and happy in Stamford. We now go to America once a year to see our families there, and we are all seeking God's will for our future.

The serious state of my health when we first returned to England can hardly be exaggerated. I was completely exhausted; 'burnt out' in the service of Jesus. I was under the consultancy of a heart specialist, and suffered constant, severe chest pains. On more than one occasion I was admitted to hospital as an emergency case. Chronically and deeply depressed, I was in a constant state of pathological anxiety, suffering severe panic attacks and phobias which included agoraphobia, and this confined me to going only short distances from our home. I had had so much 'laying-on-of-hands' ministry that it is a wonder I was not bald! And so much 'healing of memories' that I am surprised I did not forget who I was! It was all of no avail. God did not heal me.

However, one morning in March 1985 I was lying in bed, reading from the Psalms. Suddenly my eye lit upon a verse from Psalm 118. It read:

"Thou shalt not die, but live and declare the works of the Lord."

This verse seemed somehow to be flashing before my eyes, illuminated like a light bulb; nothing else seemed to be written on the page. I knew that God had spoken to me through His Word. It was a promise from Himself. I praised Him, and thanked Him aloud. The chest pains I had been enduring ceased immediately. I soon consulted the specialist, who said that I could now dispense with the "life-saving" heart medication I was taking; and I have never had a chest pain from that day to this. Examinations have shown that my heart is in very good condition.

In June 1988 the psychiatrist I was consulting retired, and a new, younger doctor took his place. He immediately prescribed new medication to control my chemical imbalance. After taking this for several days I awoke one morning to what seemed a new world, with new hope. I must, it seems, apart from a miraculous intervention, take this medication in larger or smaller doses, depending upon my state of health, for the rest of my life. I feel that God has helped me through the medical profession.

My health, however, is very delicate and I still suffer from severe bouts of depression if I overwork. This book has, in fact, taken five years to write its few pages. Apart from the short missions to Singapore and Malaysia, and visits to Scotland and Ireland, which were by no means demanding, but left me completely exhausted and ill, I have only been able to take occasional meetings. Such efforts are deemed, by my doctor, to be therapeutic to me as long as I am extremely careful and make them only spasmodically.

On July 22nd 1995, friends of ours, Chris and Fran Oldroyd of Farnham, Surrey, organised a day of prayer and fasting for me. This involved a hundred of our prayer partners, many of whom prayed at home, but several gathered at a meeting room in Stamford to wait upon the Lord. Towards the end of this prayer meeting Anne and I went amongst them to hear what they felt God had said about our future, and also to receive ministry.

My health has improved remarkably since that time. However, the word that came through was that we should let go of our past, very demanding, itinerant ministry, and engage in much more local ministry. I am therefore now undertaking occasional ministry as an honorary associate priest at St Mary's Church, Stamford. It is an Anglo-Catholic Church, with wonderfully rich worship and an evangelical outlook. I also minister at St. Martin's Church, Stamford. The people are appreciative of my approach to Christian truth and we are hopeful about the future of my ministry there. Anne is, of course, busy in the life and service of the church, including the wider sphere of the Women's Aglow Fellowship in England, to which I am a National Adviser and which both Anne and I actively support in its valuable work amongst women.

Furthermore, we formed a nationwide network of intercessors, work that was ably co-ordinated by Mrs Stella Godsmark, who shared in our ministry to the sick in a most effective way. This work of intercessory prayer is dedicated and ongoing.

I also conduct Bible Studies, not only for St Mary's people

but also for the local Full Gospel Businessmen's Fellowship, with which organisation I have long been proud to be associated. In addition to these activities I am also an Honorary Chaplain to the healing work known as the Guild of St Luke the Physician, and Anne and I undertake healing and counselling ministry at home. I am further being called upon to be a personal consultant to Christian leaders and to write Christian books. So I am far from idle in the Lord's vineyard!

In all this, which for me is therapeutic work, we are supported in prayer and finance by a loyal band of prayer partners. I also receive disability pensions, and so the Lord has provided for us in every way. In the words of Charles Wesley:

We praise Him for all that is past
And trust Him for all that's to come.

PART FIVE

Reflections

Chapter 22

Treasure in earthen vessels

I have given a description of my Christian pilgrimage thus far and, in the last twelve years, I have had plenty of time to reflect on certain aspects of the Christian Faith and to reach definite conclusions about what I believe the God of truth has taught me.

A) THE BIBLE

From what I have seen of the truth of God as revealed in the Bible, especially as it has worked out in my own ministry, I cannot but assert that the Bible is God's word to mankind. God has used its words to speak powerfully to me for the transformation of my own life and ministry and, as I have spoken its words to seekers, many hundreds of lives have been dramatically changed and made whole through the action of the Holy Spirit. I believe therefore that all Scripture is inspired by God and the Bible contains all truths that are necessary for our salvation. Further, I believe that if a spiritual proposition cannot be proved from the Bible, then it is false and does not emanate from the God of truth.

Does this mean to say therefore that all the studies I undertook for my Bachelor of Divinity Degree at Wesley College was all so much theological garbage? No, I do not think so.* What I have learned through an academic and scholarly study of the Bible is that, although it is inspired, it contains a definite human element, which runs right through it from Genesis to Revelation. The Bible is in fact a library of books by different writers and, because in Biblical times writers often ascribed their work to famous people, authorship cannot be taken for granted. The times in which each book was written must also be taken into account when interpreting Scripture and also the fact that in those days people had a three-storey view of the universe must also be accepted. For them, heaven was above the sky, the earth was flat and held up by pillars, and 'hades', the place of the dead, was under the earth.

There are also some minor discrepancies in the different accounts, even of the life of Jesus. In all, it must be said that we have this wonderful treasure of God's Word in "earthen vessels" (2 Cor. 4 v 7, KJV). But treasure it is: the news of God's relationship of love with mankind and the action He has taken to bring us back to Himself. Human element there certainly is, but this is the Book God has given us as the ultimate truth, and it is a mine of gold for us to read, upon which to meditate and absorb into our very beings.

*(Note: The publisher wishes to make clear that she considers 'higher' and 'lower' criticism of the Bible to be extremely dubious. She finds the theses of Josh McDowell in *More Evidence that Demands a Verdict* convincing.)

B) THE CHURCH

It has been our privilege, in our ministry, to have deep fellowship with and to minister amongst Christians of all persuasions. We have served Roman Catholic Renewal Fellowships, Anglican, Methodist, Baptist, Pentecostal, and Independent Community Churches as well as speaking at Full Gospel Businessmen's dinners and teaching sessions and gatherings of the Women's Aglow Fellowship. This has been a very rich experience for us as we have seen the dedication, worship and church life of thousands of Christians. I feel, on reflection, that the simplest and yet most profound definition of a local church is described in our Lord's words that "Where two or three are gathered together in my Name, I am there in the midst of them."

What I consider to be very sad, is the way Christian denominations have, in general, become polarised in their emphasis either on the ministry of the Word in preaching, or on the Grace of God ministered through the Sacraments. This is not to say that I haven't heard some good sermons in 'Catholic' situations, or seen very deep devotion in Pentecostal Churches as they have 'broken bread' and distributed what they call the 'emblems' of bread and wine. Nevertheless the gap between 'Catholic' and 'Evangelical' traditions is very wide.

It will have become obvious to the reader, from the description of my spiritual pilgrimage, that I cannot feel myself to be other than a Pentecostal, Evangelical Christian of Anglo-Catholic persuasion, and that the church where I felt all these elements came beautifully together was at St Luke's, Seattle. I am sure that St Paul was also of such a persuasion, as he emphasised the reality of the Body of Christ in the Lord's Supper (1 Cor. 11), preached for the conversion of unbelievers, and the edification of Christians and yet emphasised the place of the gifts of the Holy Spirit in the Church (1 Cor. 12).

We have also appreciated in our ministry the wonderful worship, praise, adoration and thanksgiving through new spiritual songs, usually accompanied by a worship group of musicians and singers, and also the deep sense of belonging to each other, of the new churches which usually meet in public halls or schools. How we have wished that these elements of church life could permeate the more traditional churches, whereby the 'church' is usually understood as meaning the building in which each member comes to perform their individual act of devotion and to receive their personal grace. Thankfully, in the Charismatic Renewal movement, the elements of joyous praise and a sense of Christian community have spilled over to some degree into renewed denominational congregations, especially as 'house meetings' and 'Celebration' gatherings have become more common. The more Catholic churches however, have much to teach these groups about the value of silence, Quiet Days and Retreats.

We are sure that it takes all the emphases of church life which we have experienced to make up the richness of the universal Church and we do hope that as Christians fellowship together and they are renewed by the Holy Spirit, the richness of each grouping will be shared, to make a New Testament expression of Church life a reality.

As it is at present, the universal Church is divided into what we call denominations. Even Community Churches are forming such denominations as they place themselves under what they consider to be 'Apostolic' ministries (example -- the New Frontiers grouping under Terry Virgo). Also local churches are usually far from perfect, often having inner disharmonies amongst the members. In this respect, again, the new Community Churches, in our experience, are not immune from the problem and have, at times, been so divided that whole groups have left them to form their own, separate church. As with the Bible, there is treasure in the Church, and this treasure is contained in "earthen vessels". However, all who seek for Christ can find Him in some part of His Church and will find that the Church will be a means of Grace to nurture their Christian life.

C) THE CHRISTIANS

In our travels we have had not only fellowship but also long conversations with scores of Christians, and we have always been interested in hearing the story of their spiritual pilgrimage. We have also counselled many people about their relationship with Jesus. I have heard 'confessions' and, particularly at Full Gospel Businessmen's meetings, have heard detailed testimonies about how men came to know Jesus. In all this, there have never been two stories alike. My own initial encounter with Christ was, as I have said, dramatic when I was in desperate need of healing. On the other hand, Anne cannot remember a time when she was not conscious of the existence of God and His interest in her. What then makes a person a Christian in the beginning?

Catholic, Sacramental churches emphasise that we become Christians at our baptism, even though this be as babies, when we cannot be conscious of Jesus and what He has done for us. Evangelicals on the other hand emphasise the paramount import-ance of a conscious and deliberate putting of our trust in Jesus as our Saviour from sin, at which time, they teach, we are 'born again' of the Holy Spirit. I first met this Evangelical teaching at Cliff College, where it was emphasised that this experience was always so dramatic that we would be able clearly to remember it and even name the occasion on which it happened.

Certainly, the New Testament teaches that personal faith in Jesus and baptism into Him are both important. However, experience has taught us that unlike what Evangelicals believe, it is not important which in fact comes first. 'Charismatics' generally take this point of view, emphasising that to be a Christian we must have a personal relationship with and exper-ience of Jesus, by whatever means this comes about. This is in fact my own point of view.

For those brought up in Christian homes, and taught the faith from early years, 'confirmation in the faith' will certainly not be as dramatic an experience as 'conversion to the faith'. Those who have always endeavoured to live according to Christ's teaching will not experience as great a change in their lives as converts from other religions, or no religion at all. Also people who have lived in ways that are far removed from Christianity will experience a dramatic change as they 'turn to Christ'.

In any case becoming a Christian, however our experience began, is a life-long process. We are saved by Jesus on the Cross; we are saved when we put our trust in Him, and St Paul bids us still to 'work out our salvation with fear and trembling' (Philipp.

2 v 12). There are also degrees of commitment to Christ, such as the call to 'full surrender' to which I responded at Cliff College. This certainly deepened my experience of Jesus, as did my 'baptism in the Holy Spirit' in 1969. These 'crisis' experiences however, real though they were, have been no substitute for my growth in the knowledge and love of Jesus which, I hope, has gone on ever since.

In the end our knowledge and experience should cause an increase of release, joy and peace as we know the answer to the questions:

"Who am I?" *answer*   -- a child of God
"Why am I here?"   -- to love and serve Him
"Where am I going?"   -- to a glorious eternal destiny

The purpose of man is, through Jesus, truly known to us -- to love, serve and enjoy God here on earth and live with Him for ever in heaven.

In my experience being a Christian should certainly give us a positive attitude to life. Sadly we have met some Christians who are so introspective about their Christian life and even afraid of disobeying God, that they have become analytical, depressed, negative and unhappy. This we have found to be far more common in Charismatic-Evangelical circles than in Catholic expressions of the Faith.

Obviously, these depressed people have got something wrong in their relationship with God. Some have even become pathologically ill. St John stated: "perfect love drives out fear," and these folk need a lot of re-educating about the Christian way. In the end, judgement about who are, or who are not, true Christians is God's affair and not ours. Our task is to keep on sharing our experience of Jesus with others and leave the spiritual work of a call to conversion or consecration to the Holy Spirit. However, Jesus told us that the true mark of a Christian is not their profession (saying to Him 'Lord, Lord') or the power of their ministry (prophecy or casting out demons in His Name), but the 'fruit' which their lives bear (Matt. 7).   Ultimately therefore, although we shall always carry our treasure in earthen vessels and be imperfect, what matters is not what we say or do (though these are important), but the quality of a Christ-like life, and this quality is the ultimate witness to the reality of Christian Faith.

D) BAPTISM IN THE HOLY SPIRIT

I have described my experience of what is generally called the 'Baptism in the Holy Spirit' earlier in this book. It certainly revolutionised my Christian life and ministry. This, as I have recounted, also happened to Anne as she sought the blessing. The promise was first made by John the Baptist, who said of Jesus: "He is the One who will baptise you with the Holy Spirit," (Matt. 3 v 11; Mark 1 v 8; Luke 3 v 16; John 1 v 33). Christians of the early Church also experienced a mighty in-filling of the Spirit before they were able to begin their powerful ministry (Acts).

As we have travelled around we have found that this experience is not for the chosen few, but for *every Christian* who asks for it. Often however, it seems that this infilling is received in a less dramatic way than either Anne or I exper-ienced, but the result is the same; a strengthening and deepening of our relationship with God, and an intensifying of our Chris-tian experience and service. In brief, it can be said according to the testimonies we have heard, that the Baptism of the Holy Spirit results in:

A deeper awareness of the presence of Jesus

A greater expectancy of what He will do

A clearer hearing of the Voice of God

Deeper understanding of the Holy Scriptures

Freedom in testifying to others about our relationship with Jesus

Greater liberty in praise and worship

A penetrating insight into the reality of evil forces and Jesus' victory over them

Entry into the realm of supernatural gifts of the Holy Spirit (1 Cor. 12)

Greater reality in one's praise life and one's communion with God

More effective ministry for the Lord

In our experience the reception of this infilling of the Spirit is usually, but not always, accompanied by the reception of the gift of an unknown tongue. Certainly, in any case, the receiver should notice one or more of the differences I have enumerated in their walk with the Lord.

No Christian can be said to be without a measure of life in the Spirit, because Paul teaches that no one can say, "Jesus is Lord", except by the Holy Spirit. It is possible also that a Christian may receive the gift of the fullness of the Spirit accompanying their conversion to Christ, as did the household of Cornelius (Acts 10). However one receives, and at whatever time, life in the Holy Spirit is not meant to be a static condition for any Christian. We must, as the Bishop used to pray over each candidate at the Anglican Confirmation Service, "Increase in the Holy Spirit more and more until we come to God's everlasting Kingdom".

Through this infilling our bodies become, states St Paul, "Temples of the Holy Spirit" (1 Cor. 6). However, this does not guarantee us any kind of perfection. This temple is still earthly, or to use Paul's words, it is still an "earthen vessel". We are still therefore liable to sin or fall into error. However, the blessing of being so filled by the Holy Spirit cannot be exaggerated. It is a treasure beyond price, earnestly to be sought.

E)   THE GIFTS OF THE HOLY SPIRIT

The present renewal or 'Charismatic' movement is so called because of a new emphasis on the 'charismata' -- the gifts of the Holy Spirit.   The re-discovery has been made of the value of these gifts in the life of the Christian and his service for the Kingdom, and for the Church as a whole.   By far the most common gift I have found to be in evidence amongst 'Charismatic' or 'Pentecostal' Christians of all denominations, is the **gift of tongues** (1 Cor. 12).   This is primarily for use in one's personal devotions, being a vehicle, beyond natural under-standing, of communion with and prayer to God.   It breaks through the language barrier.

However, as St Paul taught (1 Cor. 14) and as we have experienced, it is also for use when the Church is gathered, as a way God speaks to His assembled people, either as a whole, or in small groups.   On such occasions it is always to be followed by the use of a second spiritual gift, that of **interpretation** (not translation), so that the listeners may understand, in their own language, what God is saying to His people.   Often, in inspired worship, the congregation also actually sings in tongues, praising God in worship where neither the words nor the tune have been learned.   It is a beautiful and moving sound.

The utterance of the interpretation of tongues is very akin to the use of the gift of **prophecy**, through which again God speaks to His people about His will, His promises or His purpose.   This gift is also common in renewal congregations where God is actually given an opportunity to speak through periods of silence, especially during times of worship.   The utterance can include a *fore*-telling or, as is more usual, is an act of '*forth*-telling' as the prophet speaks what he or she feels is the mind of God.

Of great use in the individual's spiritual life is the gift of **faith**, which Jesus said can move obstacles which are blocking

God's will, even if they be as big as mountains (Mark 11). Faith, which is of paramount importance in the Christian life is always, in Scripture, seen to be the gift of God (Eph. 2 v 8). However, there are, it seems, different degrees of faith, and Christians should always be asking, from the Holy Spirit, for a greater measure of this precious gift.

The gift of **knowledge** -- knowing that of which one would naturally be ignorant, is also in our experience much used amongst Charismatic Christians. It is of great importance when counselling, as through it one can have supernatural knowledge about the real cause of a person's problems. However, in renewed churches it is primarily used in relation to the receiving of healing from God, as the symptoms and nature of a particular person's sickness are supernaturally received by another Spirit-filled Christian who is present. I have discovered, however, that the recounting of such knowledge does not guarantee healing from God, but it is often a decisive stimulant to faith for the sick person who receives the word of knowledge as for himself.

The **discerning of spirits** is a supernatural insight into the presence of evil spirits in a person or a building, and also an exact knowledge of the nature of the evil. It is a necessary prerequisite to exorcism or deliverance ministry, which is widely exercised in renewal churches. As with the gift of healing, I will give my further reflections about this later.

The gift of the utterance of a word of **wisdom** (first seen in Scripture as an endowment given to Solomon, but then supremely in the teaching of Jesus) is not as much emphasised in these days as it should be. However, I have often been amazed at the spiritual wisdom of seemingly new, Spirit-filled Christians, which I have felt exceeded all I have learnt in my theological education!

The final gift that I will consider which is enumerated by Paul in his first letter to the Corinthians (Chap. 12) is that rare endowment of the ability to work **miracles**, and involves being able to meet needs, or further the Kingdom of God, by acts which supersede the constraints of nature (eg Jesus' feeding of the five thousand [John 6], or turning water into wine [John 2]). I have heard testimonies about, for instance, Christians repairing car engines by the laying-on of hands, but they have not been personally witnessed by myself.

The only time I have been able to use this gift was when, in answer to a need, as was the case with Jesus' miracles, I prayed for this gift, and was then able to start a car with a Yale front-door key. For the owner had lost the ignition key; but even this, although the husband of the lady concerned found it impossible to insert the front-door key into the ignition next morning, could be disputed as a 'miracle'.

These *supernatural* gifts of the Spirit (1 Cor. 12) are the ones being emphasised in our own ministry and are what we have discovered in our fellowship with renewal churches. However, none of them, whether prophecy or interpretation of tongues, words of knowledge or of wisdom, is infallible. They are being used by human beings, who, despite being filled with the Spirit, can sometimes get things wholly or partly wrong, no matter how sincere they may be. All spiritual gifts have to be tested against Scripture and by their results. Paul went on from his enumeration of spiritual gifts (1 Cor. 12) to talk about the more excellent way of love (1 Cor. 13). So the possession of spiritual gifts is no guide to the user's spiritual maturity and certainly not to infallibility. They are gifts which are given by the Grace of God for the building up of His Church, received and used by faith. We have this treasure in earthen vessels.

F)   THE MINISTRY OF DIVINE HEALING

It will be obvious from the story of our ministry that Anne and I have been much used by God in the ministry of

Divine healing. In fact I have only given a sample of the many healings which we have had reported to us by word, letter or through newspaper articles. Obviously whilst I was Vicar of St Paul's, Hainault, and Rector of St Luke's, Seattle, we were located for a while in one place and therefore in a much better position to see long-term healing than when we were engaged in an itinerant ministry. Since that time we have been constantly moving on as only visitors to churches, and we have had to rely on pastors or people who have been healed finding out our address and writing to us about what God had done through us on each specific visit. It must be stated that a pastoral situation of a healing ministry presents more challenges than an itinerant one, because then the resident minister has to care for the unhealed, whereas an evangelist just moves on. This brings us to the point as to why some people are healed by God and some are not.

There are, sadly, many extreme points of view in Charismatic circles about the reason for Christians remaining unhealed. I heard one internationally known minister of Divine healing say that if a Christian remained sick, then he or she was either in sin or in ignorance. Others, especially Christian ministers in America, put all the onus for being healed on the faith of the recipient, and teach that a sick person should ignore symptoms and keep on confessing that they have been healed even when they are still sick. One lady, who followed a brand of this teaching, told me when receiving ministry from me, that she had been already "healed in the heavenlies", but was waiting for the physical, earthly, manifestation of her healing to take place. All this contradicts the explicit accounts of immediate healing which took place in New Testament times, as recorded in the Bible.

I have certainly grappled with the problem of the unhealed and been very concerned about it ever since I began my healing ministry. I have seen many people of undoubted faith continue sick or even die young, whilst continually availing themselves of my ministry. I have not been able to accept teaching that they lacked the faith to be healed and felt it to be very unfair even to hint that this may be the case. I have not been able to accept either that they must have had some other blockage such as bitterness, unforgiveness or resentment which hindered God working in their lives. Surely when Jesus healed every single person of the crowds that came to Him, all were not in a perfect spiritual state in which to receive His healing touch.

Of some consolation is the fact that there are hints of failure to bring immediate healing even in the ministry of St Paul. In his letter to the Philippians he states that his fellow-worker Epaphroditus was "ill, and almost died" and goes on to say, not that Epaphroditus got greater faith, or confessed that he was well, but that "God had mercy on him". Further, Paul says he had to leave Trophimus behind him sick, and the apostle urges Timothy to take "*a little wine* because of your stomach and your *frequent illnesses*". No! Divine healing is a Sovereign act of God, and why He doesn't heal on every occasion, until a person has reached a ripe old age, is a mystery.

Personally, I have felt, certainly in comparison to the ministry of Jesus and even the apostles, that my ministry has always been imperfect. I have, with Anne, a gift of healing which has often been manifested, but we have always had, and will continue to have this treasure in "earthen vessels". The Church, as a corporate body, is also far from perfect in faith and in the power of the Spirit, and we live in an unbelieving world which constantly encroaches on our spiritual lives. The devil also is still very powerful in what he can inflict on believers, and we don't always obtain victory over him. In all this I often wonder that anyone is healed at all through our, or anyone else's ministry. However, we continue to offer the best we have to God and to the sick and give God all the glory when miracles take place, for we believe that healing, whether medical or spiritual, is in the end His work.

TREASURE IN EARTHEN VESSELS

G) THE MINISTRY OF DELIVERANCE

This ministry is generally called 'exorcism', especially by the media. However, I have only used this particular designation when I have been dealing with a person who is actually 'possessed' (Greek: ruled), rather than a sufferer who is afflicted, tormented, or oppressed by an evil spirit. In the latter, less serious cases, I prefer the word 'deliverance'.

It is clear that I have had to minister either deliverance, or occasionally exorcism, on many occasions. I have usually done so in healing meetings when I have actually discerned that I have been dealing directly with the devil or his minions. This has always been with people who have been involved in the occult, or have given themselves continually to deliberate sin, such as prostitutes or drug addicts. Sometimes I have discerned that alcoholism or homosexuality has been directly caused by satanic power.

The ministry of Jesus was, according to John, to "destroy the devil's work" (1 John 3 v 8) and, in the Gospels, He is recorded as bringing deliverance to at least one man who was emotionally deranged, and to others who had physical symptoms, such as a case of blindness, epilepsy, or a man who was deaf and dumb, which Jesus discerned were caused by 'demons' or 'unclean' spirits. However, as with the ministry of healing, I would want to distance myself from extremes of teaching and practice which are current in charismatic circles today.

We have had to deal, in fact, with several cases of people who suffered at the hands of contemporary 'deliverance ministries'. One young lady, a lovely Christian, sought out help because she had been told by one who ministered deliverance that she was possessed by the spirit of 'Jezebel', which was too strong for them to exorcise. Another casualty who came to us was a man confined to a wheelchair who, despite the fact that he loved the Lord, was told he was possessed by the spirit of 'antichrist'. That particular centre believes apparently also in possession of victims by a so-called 'strong man', who, like Jezebel and antichrist, has to be expelled before any further deliverance can take place. Some sufferers are wrongly anointed with consecrated Communion wine to expel spirits by would-be exorcists. Other extremes we have encountered are:

> A woman who was having a nervous breakdown being exorcised, which ministry only made her worse.
>
> A woman who wanted to break from Valium being exorcised of a 'pharmaceutical' spirit, which was of no avail.
>
> An overweight woman being exorcised of a demon of 'obesity' -- she continued to put on weight.
>
> A woman who was exorcised of 'the demon of the fear of spiders' -- all to no avail.

And so I could go on, because some ministries seem to consider every conceivable affliction as a 'demon' from which the sufferer needs to be delivered. The result is often that the person has to undergo many hours of so-called deliverance ministry, in some cases on many occasions, all of which prove to be ineffective in bringing relief. Sometimes scores of so-called 'demons' are cast out, one after another, leaving the 'afflicted' person traumatised and weak. All this is contrary to the New Testament pattern, where the spirits, no matter how many, all go immediately at a word of command, either by Jesus Himself, or the word uttered in His Name.

Once again, as with healing, I myself would not claim to have had a perfect ministry in this respect, as my gift of 'discernment' of affliction being caused by evil spirits has been subject to my human fallibility, but I have always tried to follow the New Testament pattern of ministry. When this has not been instantaneously successful I have felt that the problem must have other causes, which I have sought by counselling the patient and in prayer. My conclusion is that deliverance or exorcism ministry is a valid ministry for today, but it must be preceded by true discernment and in all respects conform to the New Testament example.

CONCLUSION

Christianity is a religion. However, it is different from other world religions in that the worship of God and obeying the laws He has given are not deemed to be matters only of outward observance, but to spring from motivation from the heart. Jesus said that those who worship God must worship Him "in Spirit and truth" (John 4 v 24), and He enunciated God's commandments as loving Him with "heart, mind, soul and strength, and in loving one's neighbour as oneself". Going beyond that Jesus said, "I give you a new commandment. Love each other as I have loved you" (John 15 v 12).

So being a Christian involves a whole transformation of one's life from primarily loving oneself, which is the essence of the Christian concept of 'sin', to loving God and one's fellow men and women in a way that Jesus demonstrated and taught love to be.

I would go even further by saying, as I did in the introduction to this book, that God whom our Lord Jesus Christ revealed, is the true God; because, through the Holy Spirit, His promises to mankind do in fact **work out** in practice. Wherever Jesus ministered, there were results in the transformation of human lives in spirit, mind and body. Further, He actually sent out His disciples on the first Christian mission with the command to "preach the Gospel, heal the sick and cast out demons" (Luke 9). Results to this effect accompanied their proclamation of the nature of the true God of love and power.

Those results are further evidenced in the mission of the early Church as recorded in the Acts of the Apostles. It was said of these first Christians, "Those who have turned the world upside down, have come here also". Is this still true today in our modern scientific and technological society? Does God still

172

reveal Himself as the true God by the results which accompany entering His Kingdom? I believe that He does.

I have described how I became a Christian after being brought up with very little exposure to the faith. I first experienced God as One who heals the afflicted in mind and body. There were immediate results of believing which were evidenced in my life. I have described how God spoke to me at Cliff College, calling me fully to surrender my life to Him. Again, there were results in my spiritual pilgrimage. I have described my ministry, at first very frustrating, but then, after receiving the baptism of the Holy Spirit, quite dynamic. Anne's life was also revolutionised by her commitment to Jesus and eventual reception of an infilling of spiritual power.

Before this experience we both tried to minister in our own strength. After it, we saw the results in peoples' lives as promised by Jesus. We have seen God to be true to His Word. We saw also transformed, loving Christian churches at St Paul's, Hainault, and St Luke's, Seattle, as the believers fully surrendered themselves to God and received the fullness of the Holy Spirit.

All this has not, as I have stated, been without problems. We have seen many believers remain unhealed and struggle with emotional problems. We have had doubts about extreme teachings which have seemed to affirm all manifestations of the charisma and powerful ministries to be, as it were, infallible. We have also had difficulty with exaggerated claims that whenever results have not been forthcoming the fault lies somehow with the seeker of God's blessing and healing. We have also had problems with extremes of deliverance ministries, which have resorted to non-scriptural teaching and means of expelling supposed demons. Also, I myself became sick and, despite much ministry of laying-on of hands, inner healing and attempts at deliverance, remained exhausted and prone to bouts of serious depression. I have had times, in depression, when I have doubted even God's existence and questioned whether Christianity is not a delusion. At such times, I have been brought through again to faith by the wonderful love, support and uncomplicated faith of my beloved wife Anne.

I have, during the last dozen or so years, when well, given a lot of time to serious reflection on all I have experienced and seen of God's loving work in my own life and our joint ministry. It is too real to be doubted by any normal person. God is the God of truth. However, if man searches for infallible truth this side of heaven he is bound to be disappointed, because we have this treasure in earthen vessels. I believe the Bible has a human element, the Church is definitely fallible, the ministry of even the most gifted servant of God is fallible; I am fallible! However, even in our small ministry when God has broken through our fallibility, He has truly shown Himself to be the God of truth in whom we can put our trust in time and eternity.

If you haven't already done so, commit yourself, all you have, are and ever hope to be, into His loving hands. Fully surrender to Him. Be filled with the Spirit (Eph. 5 v 18) and you will find Him to be a life-transforming presence in your own life and in the lives of others as you reach out in faith to them to share the glorious news of the Gospel.

Publisher's note

Since this edition of *It's True!* was published, God granted the much prayed-for healing of the author. In response particularly to the prayers of many who united on 22nd July 1997 to pray, the Lord wonderfully touched Trevor and restored him to full health and strength.

Although at first he was careful not to take on too many commitments, he subsequently found that his strength was renewed in such a way that he has been fully engaged in the healing/evangelistic ministry as before. So the Lord continues to bless Trevor as he serves Him, together with Anne, in the power of the Holy Spirit.